"Michael McIntyre has tirelessly spent time helping people get to their next level in life, business, and focus. In comes his book which is appropriately named after his life mission: *the Next Level Life*. This is a work where he candidly tells his own story about growing from a hustling young businessman trying to set some major goals for success, to the up and down journey of life which lead him to his extremely rooted marriage, his conversion to Christianity and all that it contributed to him, to recreating his success again through another business. Sometimes a person's story can preach louder than fifty self help books, and that's exactly what Michael accomplished here. Get the book. Then get coached by Michael and his organization."

—SHAWN BOLZ
Best Selling Author, TV Host,
Podcaster, Husband, and Father
www.bolzministries.com

"Michael McIntyre is a deep well. He is hilariously funny, and his quotes will stay with you and change your life experience. In his latest book *Next Level Life* you will see how God had His hand on McIntyre all of his life and allowed him to rise from a life of hardship to building a successful multi-billion dollar business. When Michael thought he had it all, Jesus interrupted him and changed the trajectory of his life. His work is truly a rags to riches story, and Michael's passion now is helping others with his *Next Level Experience*. He is a coach, author, speaker and all around great guy. This book is a must read."

—BOB HASSON
CEO HPCI, author, speaker, consultant
www.bobhasson.com

"Michael McIntryre's memoir, *Next Level Life,* is a gripping rags to riches story told with honesty and humor. It is a page turner of an adventurous life, both well-lived and well-learned. His journey of navigating the difficulties and joys of growing a billion-dollar enterprise is both compelling and hilarious. In his usual style, he is a coaching storyteller. You will glean tremendous wisdom and lessons from the pages of his life. The bonus of all is his supernatural awakening with Jesus that took him from a 2-dimensional life and accelerated his huge personality and life impact into a 3-dimensional life. He still runs at the same speed and effectiveness but now is impacting the earth through the kingdom. The sound of his life is echoing in heaven."

—TRACY ECKERT
Senior Pastor of *Storehouse Church*, Dallas
www.tracyeckert.com

NEXT
LEVEL
LIFE

a memoir

NEXT LEVEL LIFE

a memoir

———

MICHAEL MCINTYRE

I dedicate this memoir to my wife, Stacye, and our three daughters, Brittany, Brianna, and Brecca.

CONTENTS

FOREWORD

They say, *behind every successful man is a woman*. Behind Michael, there are four.

Of the four, our mother is the best. Truly. She has given Michael the wings to do the things he knew he was meant for.

If you are the 1% who are reading this foreword, before reading the rest of Michael's story, I want to share with you *our perspective* (referring to my sisters and I). We have great respect for our father and the way in which he honestly lets you into his life and thoughts.

To return to my first sentiment, when I tell you that my father has four women behind him, I mean it! He should win a Nobel peace prize for the ways in which he has humbled himself before the girls in his life. He has allowed us to teach him things that many men would ignore. It is *our honor* to be his daughters.

As you read about Michael's inner workings, know that all throughout fatherhood, he has been a man of great integrity and honor. There is no better picture of his life's fruit than how much we all adore him.

My dad and mom have sacrificed everything for us girls. When I began working with them over seven years ago, I was overcome with a deep sense of gratitude. I began to grasp the extent of their fight and the perseverance they have maintained throughout my life, all while showing us so much love and grace in the process.

We all hope to make them as proud as they have made us.

To whet your appetite for the story that you are about to read—I will leave you with the quote that most reminds me of Michael:

"The reasonable man adapts himself to the world: the unreasonable one persists in trying to adapt the world to himself. Therefore all progress depends on the unreasonable man" (George Bernard Shaw).

—BRIANNA MCINTYRE
Daughter & COO of *McIntyre*

CHAPTER ONE

FLINT

I HAD SPENT two decades building a 3-billion dollar company, and it was finally time to turn off the lights. I would like to tell you it was a dramatic, Hollywood-style farewell when I left my office for the last time—but it wasn't. I generally don't do *goodbyes,* and exiting a 9+ figure venture was no exception. Like a game of Monopoly, my time as CEO probably went on a little longer than it should have and was starting to cause more stress than it was worth. I did not realize it then, but selling off the company could not have come at a sweeter time. It was 2007.

Leading up to this, our revenue was great. We had taken the economic downturn following 9/11 on the chin and had bounced back in big ways. The bank account was full, but my heart was somehow still empty. I worked in a premiere section of Dallas in a glass-walled corner office. Meanwhile, my heart was anything but premiere. It was desolate. Perhaps that was not obvious to everyone else—it's not like I was walking around on suicide watch.

Nobody was hiding the shotgun or leading me away from ledges, but you don't have to be at that place to know something is missing in your life. Fixing this *fulfillment crisis* was something they had not taught me in college, the military, or Catholic school, for that matter. Regardless, I do not want to bog you down with my labor pains. I'd rather just show you the baby.

Someone recently asked me, "Did you ever think you would be as successful as you became?" With the risk of sounding arrogant, my answer was, "Yes." When people experience success, they often look back and think, *I never imagined that I'd end up here!* Because of the hand they were dealt or the odds they faced, they cannot help but feel surprised when they end up with the 'W' at the end of the game. For me, success was not necessarily a shock. I had *visualized* it and was able to *actualize* it. If you are doing it right, success should *shadow* you, not *shock* you.

Despite having a broken home and seeing my fair share of dysfunction, which we will talk about later, I always chased success in one way or another. For as long as I can remember, I have wanted to succeed. The only thing I can compare it to is choosing your favorite color. If I asked you, "What is your favorite color?" you might say *blue.* If I asked you, "When did you decide on blue being your favorite color?" you would probably struggle to answer. It has just always been your favorite, hasn't it? Certain things in our lives are simply *inherent*.

For me, the idea of achieving my dreams seems to have been one of those inborn instincts. Now, I can't take full credit for that, as if I were some child prodigy. I wasn't. It was a cocktail of decent DNA, learned work ethic, and *grace*. There were critical moments in my youth that stoked the fire for me.

One of my first experiences with this came in 4th grade at Holy Rosary Catholic School in Eastern Michigan. As private schools often do, they put on a fundraiser for us students to be a part of. The goal was to sell as many light bulbs as possible. The student with the most sales would earn a coveted U.S. savings bond but, most importantly, *prestige*. The sexy title of *lightbulb salesman of the year* was a status I was after. For reasons only God knows, I had a knack for selling these light bulbs. I went door to door, and the sales kept coming in. I don't remember having a polished pitch or a revolutionary technique. I just remember putting in the hours to outsell everyone else.

Amid this fundraiser, I had a *lightbulb moment*, pun very much intended. It so happened that big box stores were just coming into vogue during this period in the late 1960s. At that time, to gain entry to a Costco-type wholesaler, you had to have a bonafide small business. They didn't give membership cards out to just anybody as they do now. My mother worked for Fisher Body, a division of GM, and was a union member. Labor unions are to Michigan what salt is to the ocean. They are everywhere, and the union was a quasi-mafia, in that members took care of their own. My mother knew someone in the union who knew someone else who had a card, so we got into one of these exclusive wholesale stores.

I remember seeing mountains of lightbulbs in the store and thought, *I bet I could sell my bulbs to the store and not have to go door to door. They could put in an order for $10,000 in bulbs, and my quota will be more than covered!* With my business-to-business strategy in mind, I approached the manager, introduced myself, shook his hand, and began my pitch. I was talking up the deal, and the manager's interest was piqued. Just when he started asking about specific numbers, my mom found me and said, "Michael! We're leaving. Get in the car!" I was on the edge of closing this guy, and she pulled me back from the brink of success! I was crushed. Nevertheless, I dusted myself off, and my business-to-consumer, door-to-door campaign was back in action. Door after door, my order sheet was filling up.

As we sat in class after the fundraiser had ended, an announcement came over the PA system. "We want to let you know the results of the annual lightbulb sale. In first place, the student with the most sales was Mike McIntyre." I heard my name associated with first place, and *I liked it.* Then, everyone in the class turned around and looked at me, and *I loved it.* It was the first dose of *acknowledgment* I had ever received, and it was intoxicating. My name being praised over a PA is something that no other student in that class remembers today, but for me, it was a defining moment. The first place title, the acclaim, the acknowledgment, the recognition—it all ran through my veins like a drug.

The next part was almost as sweet—proudly claiming my $50 savings bond. I thought I was rich until I cashed the thing and only got $37.50 back. Despite the $12.50 penalty for early cashing, I walked away with a newfound love for sales and making money. I was hooked! It was the start of my All-American success story, brought to you by humble beginnings in Flint, Michigan.

- - -

When I was born in the fall of 1960, Flint was actually a prosperous and happening town. People did not recoil at the name *Flint, Michigan,* as they do now. The water was drinkable and the population had just hit its peak at 200,000 people, making it the second-largest city in Michigan at the time. The town was chock full of folks in the *United Auto Workers Union,* and they remained steady until the downward slide of the auto industry.

With my mother, many family members, and 85% of the Flint population being tied to the auto industry, we felt firsthand the peaks and valleys of Michigan manufacturing. The 1973 energy crisis, oil embargo, and the inception of the oil cartel (OPEC) all created a true flashpoint for the auto industry. Yet, I wouldn't hear of those things until I was entering my teen years. Until then, GM and others provided steady, reliable work throughout the '60s.

The city was growing and expanding. With a housing shortage, those who could afford it moved to suburbs like Grand Blanc, Davison, Swartz Creek, and Flushing. Both of my parents were Flint natives. My dad, Richard J. McIntyre, was raised in Michigan. *Raised* might not be the best word to describe his upbringing. His father had left at an early age, leaving my dad and his three siblings with their mother. Their mother, my grandma, was a Cherokee Indian who had a severe drinking problem that eventually left her incapable of raising her own children. This in turn led to my dad and his siblings being brought up at Whaley Orphanage in Flint. Being an orphan carries enough baggage to write a book on, and my father was no exception. To his credit, he was able to bootstrap a decent life for himself, in spite of the hand he was dealt.

With a Catholic background and a name like *McIntyre*, it doesn't take a detective to figure out that I have a Scotch-Irish ancestry. My father was a *Scotch McIntyre* and my mother was an *Irish Kennedy.* Born Annette Teresa Kennedy, my mother was the second oldest of seven children. Her mother was a hard-working, French Canadian bookkeeper. As a bookkeeper, she was working outside the home, which was not the norm at that time. Her father ran a decently successful body shop. Unfortunately, he was an alcoholic and a violent father at that. This, of course, ensured that the family would never be short on dysfunction. Raised in this setting, my mother had a natural perseverance about her, which she would need greatly as the years passed.

Two years into the Korean conflict, which was 1952, my father joined the Marines. After being stationed in California for a season, he was sent to fight the war and returned in 1955. I do not have any battle stories from him to share, but I suppose that is fitting for a member of the "silent generation." Around the time he was returning to the States, my mother had her first child, Mel, in her first marriage. It was not until three years later, in 1958, that she and my father met on a blind date and were married shortly after.

For a brief stint, they lived in California as newlyweds. In fact, I was conceived in California, and during the pregnancy, they moved to Flint, where I was born. Flint is no Los Angeles. I would have appreciated them staying on the coast, but instead wound up in a town with a summer that lasts five days. There was nothing unusual surrounding my debut, other than the fact that I was a 10-pound 10-ounce baby. I'm told my eyes were not visible for about six months, on account of my chubby face.

At about this time, Dad worked like crazy as a debt collector while getting his education from the University of Michigan. With a half Cherokee mom, he was able to snag a scholarship to help with tuition. When I found out about that later in life, I painted my face and sent a picture to the Indian bureau to try to get some cash. You might be surprised to learn that I received none.

My mom worked for Michigan Bell, or *Ma Bell* as it was usually called, as an operator during those years. My folks were a young, attractive couple who worked hard and no doubt wanted something better than what they were handed. Frankly, we had work ethic passed down to us from both sides of the family. *Lazy* was not in our vocabulary. At some point, my father left the collections agency, graduated with a degree, and went to work for Buick. He climbed the corporate ladder and became an executive purchasing agent in the company. We occupied a home in a reasonable neighborhood on Cashin Street in Flint. We were becoming a fledgling middle-class family.

During my first few years, life was about as normal as one would expect. I have all the standard memories of smiles, laughs, and playing hide-and-seek with our babysitter. My mother and her sister, my aunt Elaine, were close, and so we spent ample time at her place. Aunt Elaine had five kids of her own and we loved every minute of the chaos with cousins.

When I was three-and-a-half years old, my little brother Matthew was born. I mentioned prior that I was a ten-pounder at birth. Matt outdid me and tipped the scales at 13 pounds fresh out of the womb. He made the news for that. God bless my mother. My parents went on to have one more child together, MaryLynn, my younger sister.

Because I was born in October, a decision had to be made as to when I would start school. Rather than waiting an entire year for me to enroll, I made the cutoff and was sent to kindergarten at age four. This did not put me at a handicap—it may have even helped me in the long run, having to keep up with kids who were a year ahead of me in development. In fact, as you will soon read, being a year younger than my peers would be the least of my concerns while I was busy avoiding ruthless nuns and sneaking beer into my lunch box.

CHAPTER TWO

CASHIN STREET CHAOS

IT HAD NOT occurred to me until that moment that the ginger ale bottle in our fridge looked an awful lot like a beer bottle. I hatched a harebrained idea: *I should empty the ginger ale, fill it with beer, recap it, and take it to school.* In those days, the legal drinking age was 18 in Michigan. I was 10, but I guess I figured I was close enough. With my contraband in my lunchbox, I went to school the next day. When lunchtime came around, the nun would leave the classroom and a lunch lady would come in and oversee us as we all pulled out our pails and ate at our desks.

I had a buddy who sat behind me named McDonald. His first name escapes me, but he had red hair and a loud mouth, as I was about to find out. The lunch lady said a brief prayer and we all dug into our food. I turned to McDonald. "Hey, I've got some beer," I whispered. "Lemme taste it," he replied. He took my ginger ale, which was just ale at that point, and took a sip. What happened next blew my cover and foiled the operation completely.

He shouted, loud and proud, "I'm gonna get DRUNK!" I winced.

Right about that time, I looked, and the lunch lady was coming down our aisle like a bloodhound on a trail. She grabbed the bottle, smelled it, and proceeded to grab me by the hair on the nape of my neck and drag me to the principal's office. Going to the principal's office in a Catholic school was like going to meet God Himself. The monsignor had black garb and a vibe that was intimidating to anyone, let alone a child. When called to his office, you were basically going into the holy of holies to get a certified whoopin'. That was exactly what happened. In fact, they took me in front of the older kids, sixth graders, had me bend over, and swatted me three times with a wooden paddle. I had bruises to the tune of not being able to sit down for two days.

Today, the teacher would be arrested and the school would be shut down. It was not just physical but *emotional* abuse. It was humiliating. In fact, when my parents were informed of my misdeed, they did not have any discipline or correction to dole out. They knew that box had been checked. It was a different era, to put it mildly. From that day forward, I made a hardline personal policy to *never* take beer into a place of worship.

That incident was probably the most trouble I got into during my formative elementary years. More mischief would come later. Academically, there was nothing that suggested I would be some business mogul or a Nobel prize winner. My teachers likely thought I'd be lucky if I ended up working in a hot dog stand. I was purely average. Straight Cs was my modus operandi with an occasional B in science or history. Trigonometry may as well have been Mandarin—math was not a strong suit. Although, *money math* always clicked with me.

Comprehending and memorizing percentages, dollar amounts, and balances came easy. I can still remember exact balances from my childhood savings account. I can recall our family's phone bill to the penny from when I was 12 years old. In fact, later, when I became an executive, I used to drive my team bonkers because I would recall exact account balances from memory and catch discrepancies on the fly. Give me numbers and I'll toss out the paper. Put dollar signs in front of those numbers, and I'll become Isaac Newton on the spot.

Unfortunately, I was no genius in the classroom, and like any kid, I was pumped about summer break. During the summers, we were haunting the streets of our neighborhood from dawn until dusk. We spent a lot of time at Lake Metamora and had a few great family vacations. Our trip to Washington D.C. was unforgettable, and seeing the massive Lincoln Memorial is burned in my memory. When my grandpa moved to Florida, we visited him often and even got to experience Disney World when it first opened in 1971. *The most magical place on earth* left an impression on me as I later became a shareholder. In those days, my grandmother had remarried a Jewish guy named Meyer Heller. He had a cabin at the tip of the thumb of Michigan in Port Huron. We had some unforgettable vacations up there.

I was coming of age in the midst of the Space Race, Civil Rights Movement, and the Vietnam War, yet I was not overly concerned with any of those things. For one, I was too young to give it much attention, and second, information was still moving at tortoise speed. We didn't have news feeds in our pockets. Besides, our summers were spent building tree houses, egging *real* houses, and stealing stuff out of gardens. When we discovered that we liked the sound of water balloons hitting cars, it became a regular hobby. That is, until we inadvertently smacked a cop car. When Johnny Law threw it in reverse and came after us, we did the 40-yard dash in about 3 seconds. That dash ended abruptly when we were close-lined by a barbed-wire fence.

Needless to say, life in the neighborhood and life in our home was par for the course. Sadly, the latter was about to change. When I was eight years old, a gigantic argument broke out between my mother and father. It was a knock-down-drag-out fight. To this day, I really don't know what the fight was about. The dispute spilled out into the yard and the police were called. I recall my aunt coming across the yard and screaming at my dad, giving him the one-finger salute. The situation was ugly.

I was scared. My world was being rocked. If you have ever lived through those types of fights, you know the instantaneous insecurity it creates in you. Prior to the cops showing up, my dad was acting unusually nice to us kids. "Can I get you anything? Do you want ice cream?" Looking back, he was probably just trying to take our minds off of the trauma that was unfolding. My dad left that night, making it my first night going to bed in a broken home.

The entire ordeal was a surprise. From my perspective, there were no preliminary fights or tension in the home before the bomb went off. The next thing I remember was moving in with my grandmother, along with my mom and siblings. A divorce ensued, and frankly, I don't recall much about its details.

At the time, I had no way of grasping the effect that the divorce would have on me. In fact, in some ways, I almost favored it because of the freedom it gave me. While my parents were wrapped up in their own chaos, I could roam and do as I pleased. On the other hand, I do remember the awful nightmares and the fear of being alone in the house—a direct byproduct of brokenness. Our mom would often go out, and if she was not back quick enough, we would call the police, terrified that something happened to her. They would arrive and reassure us as we waited nervously.

If I had to identify a silver lining in the whole thing, I would say that the independence I was forced into as a child worked out in my favor in the long run as I went into the military, started a business, and built a life for myself. It also allowed me to see firsthand something that I swore to never duplicate. When Stacye and I got married, we resolved that we would stick it out *no matter what.* Now, she might cut my brake lines or poison my food, but divorce is not in the vocabulary.

This has positioned us to raise, nourish, and support our kids in ways we just couldn't if we were wrapped up in our own dysfunction. If you are a parent, one of the best gifts you can give your child is a loving marriage for them to witness. It doesn't have to be perfect—in fact, it won't be. Yet if your kids are worth fighting for, your marriage is, too.

I encourage people today, catch your kids doing something *right.* Growing up, especially after the divorce, I was generally caught doing something *wrong.* Granted, there was plenty of wrong to catch me in. However, the job of a leader is to mine the diamonds, not criticize the coal.

- - -

The fallout from the divorce lingered for years. My dad hated paying child support. My mom would haul him off to jail constantly. It was not uncommon for my mom to have me call my dad on her behalf to ask for the child support check, supposing he would be softer toward his own kid. When he hung up on me, it became clear that was not the case. On one rare occasion when the check actually arrived, I saw *Friend of the Court* and knew what it was. Wanting to surprise my mother, I baked her a cake and placed the check on top of it.

Being privy to the dysfunction in our house, a couple of nuns from Holy Rosary took a liking to me and decided to be a positive influence in my life. Sister Anita and Sister Beauchamp would pick me up and take me to the movies, the mall, or restaurants. I was met with flack from my uncles about having new girlfriends. Looking back, I can see the providence in their actions. Nobody asked them to be a light in my life; they just were.

Unfortunately, 4th grade would be my last year in private school, and my dates with the nuns would come to an end. Money was drying up because of the divorce and going to public school would be the result. I first realized things were not great financially when I saw my mom borrowing money from her brothers. At times, my shoes had no laces, which also tipped me off. My mom later had a fifth child, my sister Gerri, in a third marriage and never seemed to be able to escape the financial pressure of five children and multiple divorces. I resolved early on to never accept money struggles as a lifestyle. A smart person learns from his or her own mistakes. A genius learns from other people's mistakes.

My first year in public school was relatively good. I remember the principal well. His name was Dave Angus, a 6'8" former college basketball star. At one point, he called my mother and me into his office and said, "Thank you for being a nice young man and a good student." I realized later that Holy Rosary had probably given him a warning about me, and he was likely expecting the worst. I exceeded his expectations until a year later, when I was kicked out of school for disrespecting a teacher.

Around that time, my buddy Marc Hagel and I were playing with fire in his attic. When we left an ember unchecked, it resulted in his garage being burned down and our friendship coming to a halt. I did not wake up in the morning determined to be a menace, but to an outsider it might appear that way. Most of the trouble I got into was fairly innocent. The only intentional chaos we caused usually involved Mass. To put it mildly, my siblings and I hated going to Mass. Father Rob was older than God and not exactly *dynamic* from the pulpit. To dodge going to church, we came up with a strategy. While our mom was out late on Saturday nights, we would turn the clocks back an hour around the house. When morning came, she would take us to church, and everyone would be leaving as we were arriving. Sure, she took her shoe off and beat us with it when she found out what happened, but the beating was Disneyland compared to Father Rob's homily.

Around age 12, my dad remarried my stepmonster, I mean, *stepmother,* Betty. Years later, we reconciled and wound up having a decent relationship, but early on it was rocky. Because of Betty, I was introduced to a second religion: Baptists. She was a hardshell Baptist who would say things about Catholics like, "They aren't *born-again.*"

It felt like there was a giant gap between us devil-worshiping Catholics and the holy, upright Baptists. It all seemed so self-righteous to me.

As traumatizing as it was to be swatted in the Catholic school in front of the older kids, it did not leave a lasting mark on me as the Baptists did. Their legalism affected me much more than getting my backside lit on fire. They were staunch and narrow-minded. On the contrary, our priest would come over to the house and smoke cigarettes and drink all our booze. Now that was cool!

There were huge differences between my mom's house, where we lived mostly, and my dad's house, where we occasionally visited. My dad had moved on with Betty and wanted a new life for himself. Dad had nice things; we didn't. He had a new gorgeous house where everything was clean, excellent, and in order. Ours was not like that at all. He drove really nice cars. We drove beaters. He would say, "Don't tell your mother about this cause she'll drag me back into court." In fact, at one point, he was building a mansion and selfishly asked us to not say anything, lest he get child support pressure.

It was as if my dad was living two lives. He and Betty seemed to fantasize about a fresh start, with just the two of them. Yet they couldn't escape the reality of us pesky kids. While I appreciated the nice things my dad had, I much preferred to be with my mother. With her, I could be myself. Things around our home were fun and real. Chaotic? Yes. But *real*. I felt I couldn't be myself around my dad. It was always a bit of a performance. This wasn't the case at home with mom. Not to mention that our visits to Aunt Elaine's house seemed to add some stability and normalcy that we lacked everywhere else.

Despite dabbling with the Catholics and Baptists, I

was not a person of faith. If I had to name a religion that I adhered to as I grew up and went into business, it would be *compound interest.* Balance sheets were the holy text and my employees were my congregation. I learned early on that I could block out so much of the nonsense of my upbringing by working and making money. It was not merely an interest but an *instinct!* In fact, at the end of our street sat Weston Elementary School. In the evenings, men would gather to play pickup basketball in the gym. They needed an employee to sweep the floor and lock up so the gym could be used as a cafeteria the next morning. Given my short commute, I was the ideal candidate for the job, so the principal hired me. I was 14 at the time.

When the men finished up their games, it was their custom to give me 35 cents apiece to go to the teacher's lounge and buy them a soft drink. The wheels began turning as I saw an opportunity for profit. The next time my mother went to the wholesale store, I went with her and priced the soft drink supply. With a refund deposit on the bottle, each soft drink would cost me just 10 cents. My margins were beginning to manifest!

The very next shift, I brought my inventory and priced each drink at 25 cents, undercutting my competition. The principal who had hired me pushed back. He argued that I was stealing opportunity from the vendor who supplied the school and questioned the legality of my operation. Being quick on my feet, I reassured him, "I completely understand... *but*, I'm *not* selling these drinks during school hours. Plus, it's a bargain for you and your friends... and it helps me out." My business carried on and my bottom line grew.

CHAPTER THREE

COMING OF AGE

"YOU WOULDN'T BELIEVE the money these insurance agents are making. Some of them are bringing home $90,000 a year!" I was blown away at my dad's words as we sat across from one another at lunch. That kind of annual cash in 1970 is well over half a million dollars in today's money. Hearing *big money* and *insurance salesman* in the same sentence probably anchored itself somewhere in my psyche more than I realized.

Dad was in his late 30s after the divorce when he became an entrepreneur. It was a big leap going from a fairly cushy, stable job at Buick to starting out in a brand new field—a field that's a commission-based, eat-what-you-kill model, no less. Working in the auto industry is nothing like working in the insurance industry, so before launching his own office, he apprenticed under an agent named Bob Stamm.

Bob was a good 15 years older than my father and had ample experience. I remember my dad working really hard to study and prepare for his exam, which he passed. Pretty quickly, my dad got me my first job in the insurance business when I was just 13 years old. I wasn't selling insurance. I wasn't generating leads. I held the highfalutin role known as *head of custodial engineering.* The job description? Cleaning bathrooms at their office. I was a little self-conscious cleaning toilets there because Bob's assistants were the prettiest ladies I had ever seen. It was burned into my mind that being an agent was the golden ring of life. It meant big money and pretty ladies.

Before I was ever offered this job, or any other job I later came by, I *created* jobs for myself. You could call it a prophetic thing as the vast majority of my adult life has been spent creating jobs for myself and others. My first startup involved getting leads, converting those leads to customers, and carrying out the promised service. I had a phone put in my bedroom that cost me $8.49 per month. We called them "teenage phones" back then. It had a separate number from the main house line, allowing me to separate my personal life and business life, a necessity for a 12-year-old tycoon.

I then put an ad in the Flint Journal stating, "I will shovel *any driveway* for a flat fee of $7." In my mind, I only needed to do two driveways per month to be in the black. I projected that if I did a couple of driveways after school every day and knocked out five on the weekend, I could bring in $75 to $100 per week, which was a fortune to a kid in 1972. Given Michigan's snowy climate, customers would not be a problem. The phone rang off the hook. Every little old widow in a 10-mile radius called me. The problem was that I lacked proper equipment, to put it mildly. All I had was a small spade garden shovel.

I often traveled for work, taking the bus to my customer's houses. On one occasion, I traveled by bus and on foot for an hour to reach the job site. The driveway was an absolutely massive, circular, dirt driveway. *I guess I did say I would do **any** driveway for $7.* I had no way out. In total, the driveway took five hours to shovel. The old lady would peak out of her curtains every hour or so, probably to make sure I hadn't frozen to death like a statue. I thought surely she would offer me hot chocolate, a Coke, or a water—but those perks never came. By the time I finished, it was dark. As I approached the front door, I expected a bonus or extra pay for the time it took me. She handed me seven singles, offered a "thank you," and shut the door. *Ouch.*

The lesson was learned: invest in better equipment and always add a caveat when giving a price quote. I actually credit this snow shoveling business as the reason I became interested in sales. It taught me that if you build the right mousetrap, they will come. Sure, I could have been better prepared for the influx, but at least I had tasted the thrill of generating leads from scratch. I was readily learning that money, in its simplest form, is a reward for solving a problem for someone.

- - -

Most teenagers are students who happen to have jobs on the side. For me, I had jobs and just happened to be a student on the side. Here's what I mean: through my middle and high school years, I was always picking up work, while academics were on the back burner in every sense of the word. I was a C and D student and had no qualms about it. When my mother threatened to hold me back,

I bumped those grades up just enough to get her off my back.

I had tried a few extra-curricular activities, but nothing really stuck. In 10ᵗʰ grade, I tried out for the football team. My dad had dreams of me playing football for the University of Michigan. I was a year younger than everyone else and a late bloomer at that, so at 5'3" and 90 pounds, I wasn't exactly getting the attention of college scouts. I only got in a couple of games, so my primary position was *left out*. However, it did teach me a lot about hard work, showing up, and doing your best with what you have.

Around that same time, I joined the debate team at our school. It was then that I uncovered a gift for public speaking and directing the narrative that would later play an integral role in my life. The University of Michigan had a 2-week intensive for high school debate teams every year. To go, you had to raise money by working the concession stand at school sporting events. I did that for an entire season, and it funded the trip. We had an incredible time on campus as a team.

I was *first negative* in the debate, so I was tasked with cross-examining and picking apart the first speaker's arguments. The *first affirmative* would stand up and give their plan to save the world; then I would stand up and tear down that argument for eight minutes with the judges watching and critiquing.

It required a ton of study and preparation for each debate, but I loved the camaraderie and excitement of it all. As a debater, you had to think on your feet. Objections would come, and you had to be able to pivot and drum up a solid response. Overcoming objections later became my bread and butter in sales.

"It's too expensive, Mike."

"I agree, this is not dirt cheap... but sir, money is not your issue. The *right solution* is the issue, and it happens to be a solution we can offer you. Are you happy with your current service?"

"No, we aren't."

"Can I write up a proposal outlining why what we can offer you is not only a *better* solution but *better value* for your money? Wouldn't you rather redirect your dollars to a more fruitful place?"

"Deal."

I've had countless conversations like this. "The price is too high. I'm too uncertain. I don't know anything about your company." The list goes on. High school debates marked the start of my dabbling in objections and dialogue. So much of my life early on foreshadowed where I would eventually end up. I was unknowingly being forged for the future. So often, we think that our foundational years are a waste. What we don't realize is that the grind is often giving us a glimpse of what's to come. The boy who collected matchbox cars became the dealership owner. The girl who was team captain became a fierce CEO. The kid with LEGOs became a world-class engineer. Childhood, school, early jobs—these things do not delay the future but develop you *for* your future. The season you are in is a *cornerstone*, not a *stepping stone*. Don't skip it. Build on it.

I remember my early taste of luxury as a kid and how it fueled me to want to access that same luxury later in life. Believe it or not, it was during a trip to Mississippi with my mother. She had just gotten a $600 tax refund, and we were off to visit my Uncle Ken, who was about to leave for Vietnam. We drove down in his car and flew

back on Delta Air Lines. It was my first time on an airplane. I was so impressed by the lights, the luxury, and
the way the flight crew dressed. I thought, *I want to live
like this.* Mom would take us to nice restaurants, which
was not the norm, and I fell in love with the feeling of
it. Of course, she prepared us with a speech beforehand,
"Do you want a beating now or after dinner?" Needless to
say, we were on our best behavior in the restaurant.

These experiences planted seeds in me. I wanted an
upper-class life, and building wealth was my path to get
there. Because of this, I never saw work as a negative.
Whether I was painting an entire home for $80 or earn-
ing $10 per week helping at my uncle's bump and paint
body shop, it was money, and money was my ticket.

In fact, I spent one of the most memorable summers
of my teen years working in the Florida heat. My mom
was dating a man named Sy. He was a cool guy, had a
beautiful Cadillac, and a knack for sales. At that time, he
moved to Florida and began selling mobile home parks.
Me and Marc Hagel (of the garage fire fame) saved our
money and flew to Florida to mow yards all summer for
Sy at his properties. It was one of my best summers. I remember watching Nixon resign from that park in Florida on August 8th, 1974. When Ford took over, he said he
would not be a *model T president* but "a new Ford." Sy
loved that line.

When I came back to Michigan, life continued on as
usual. My mom was still struggling to support her many
kids and working as hard as she could. My dad was not in
the picture much, as he was growing his insurance business and living his life with Betty.

My social life was what you would expect for your average teenager. I wasn't popular, but I also wasn't *unpop-*

ular. I had girlfriends, acquaintances, and buddies and I enjoyed bonfires and parties. We drank little, smoked cigarettes a little, but overall never went off the deep end. At 16, I was a year away from graduating and got the last job I would have before leaving Michigan. Through a family friend, my cousin Evan and I got connected to a pizza shop 40 miles away, owned by a crook named Don. We ran the shop and had a great time. Don let us drive his unregistered car around, and we probably deserved more trouble than we actually got into.

I had a decent pile of money saved up at that point, but the nest egg was about to be wiped out. Throughout my adolescent years, I got along well with my siblings, except for my older brother. To be honest, I hated him during those years. He and his friends would come over to the house, smoke dope, and eat all of our food. His life began to spiral and addiction gripped him in a big way— something that would steal so much from his life over the course of time.

We needed to send him to California for rehab and my mother didn't have the money. I remember going into the bank and having tear stains on my bank book after taking out my $2,000 savings to send him to rehab. I wanted him out of the house badly enough to go through with it—but I still loved my hard-earned money and it crushed me to part with it. It was one of the final moments of dysfunction in Michigan that I would ever have to deal with. Graduation was coming, and so was my way out.

CHAPTER FOUR

LITTLE ROCK

"**DEAR MR. MCINTYRE**, after carefully reviewing your application, we regret to inform you that we are unable to offer you admission to Central Michigan University." Apparently, my grades hadn't bedazzled CMU like I thought they would. While I didn't have parental pressure to go to college, my dad certainly favored the idea—though paying for it was the furthest thing from his mind. My mom didn't care either way—and paying for it was the furthest thing from her ability.

Needless to say, I knew college would not be a free ride. Someone told me if you go into the military, you can attend any college you want to and they will help pay for it. That interested me, so I chewed on the idea. Around Christmas time during my senior year of high school, we attended a service at Holy Rosary. During church, I noticed an airman who had come home for the holidays who went up and received communion. Something was triggered in me and I thought, *I'm going to join the Air Force to get my education. Plus, I'll look good in blue!*

Shortly after, I and a friend visited the recruiter in Flint and talked to him about the process. He mentioned that he was stationed in Little Rock, Arkansas, and he noted that they had a great college program through Arkansas State University. In fact, they even had a campus on base. I called my dad and he recommended that I enlist and sign up for as many classes as I could handle. So I did. Six months prior to graduating high school, at 17 years old, I was enlisted in the United States Air Force.

After graduation, I spent the summer running, working out, and preparing myself for basic training as much as I could. I was beyond ready to leave Michigan. I had experienced more than my share of family-oriented chaos, lack, and confusion. It was time to do something new and to do it in a completely new place.

It was the first week of September in 1978 when I stepped on a plane in Detroit to fly to Lackland Air Force base in San Antonio, Texas, for boot camp, one month before my eighteenth birthday. I was excited to be there, but I was scared. I was a kid. I had heard stories of brutal boot camps. I didn't want to fail. After stepping off the bus, the drill instructor greeted us by telling us to pick up our suitcases. He then told us to set them down. We were then instructed to pick them up again. Over and over, he had us pick them up and put them down. This went on for a genuine *two hours* before we realized the goal was to get us to pick up our suitcases in unison, at the same exact time. It was a warm welcome.

Because our flight got there on Labor Day weekend, the base was virtually empty. The lack of staff meant we couldn't get a haircut nor be issued our uniforms until

Tuesday. So all weekend, when other troops would see us, they called us "rainbows" on account of our colorful civilian clothes. They would sing, "Rainbow, rainbow, don't be blue. Our recruiter screwed us too!" On Tuesday, I was thrilled to no longer be a sore thumb as I got my haircut and a uniform issued to me. The green uniform resulted in a nickname upgrade from "rainbow" to "pickle."

For many of the guys in our flight, they were there because the judge said, "You can either go to the military or go to jail," and they chose the former. Just three of us out of 400 were taking college classes alongside military service. Others were there because jobs were slim elsewhere. We all had different reasons for enlisting, but boot camp existed to chisel away the variety and make us one unified flight.

It was both scary and intense at times. The physical training could be exhausting, but the mental games were far more grueling. Running in formation is one thing. Running in formation at 4 a.m. after being chewed out is another. Finishing the run with puke on you from the guy behind you isn't pleasant. I didn't sleep much, as you might imagine. This resulted in me breaking out in boils and being miserable at times. In fact, I recall crying myself to sleep some nights—mostly out of fear. The fear, specifically, was a fear of being sent back.

We all carried a 302 form in the front of our uniforms. If an instructor pulled that form out at any point, it meant you were sent back to day one with another squad. That sounded worse than *anything* to me. I was not great at everything, but fared well overall. Because of my experience at Don's pizzeria, I handled KP (kitchen police) duty well and knew how to scrub a pan. I struggled with proper bed-making at times, but held up well physically. Weapons training was a blast, pun intended, and I earned a ribbon for excellent marksmanship.

Back home in Michigan, I'd shoot rabbits from my treehouse with a .22 as a kid. While that might have helped me prepare a little, the Air Force didn't issue piddly .22 rifles. We were shooting full auto machine guns with tracer rounds and 40 mike-mike grenade launchers. Weapons training, police training, and combat training were all enjoyable. I developed friendships pretty quickly and made some really unique memories. One of my only regrets from this time was my failure to stay connected to some of the people I met during these years.

My dad would sometimes send me letters during basic. On one occasion, it ended in humiliation. Because these letters were sent from his insurance agency office, his photograph was on the envelope with a nice letterhead. When the sergeant saw that envelope among my things, he snatched that thing and flashed it around the group. "Look here! We have a rich kid in the group! His daddy has his own picture on his envelopes!" From that point on, I was known as the rich kid. In reality, I was a broke-joke without two pennies to rub together, but that didn't change the ribbing I got.

As basic training progressed, my ignorance was about to be found out. Our drill instructor said, "Does anyone here know how to type?" I thought to myself, *It's 99 degrees in the shade and it feels like the surface of the sun outside the shade. Typing in a cool room inside sounds great. I'll do that!* I totally ignored the advice my recruiter had given me, which was, "Never. Volunteer. For. Anything." I raised my hand, "Yes, Sergeant, I can do that!" "Great, McIntyre.

You are in charge of cleaning the latrines for the next four weeks." Welcome to the Air Force.

After six weeks of boot camp and eight weeks of police academy, it was time to graduate and be stationed. Nobody from my family came to my military graduation, which I thought was the norm until I looked around and saw everyone else's parents there. My folks weren't plugged into my time in the service. In fact, on one occasion, someone stole my civilian clothes from the dryer while I was doing laundry. All I had was my military uniform to wear, so I asked my dad for $50, and based on his response, you'd think I asked for a kidney. He was tighter than bark on a tree.

Regardless, I had pretty well been conditioned to expect these things. I was just glad to have graduated. Because my recruiter had spoken highly of Little Rock, I put in to be stationed there, and to my delight, the request was accepted. Shortly after, I moved to Jackson Air Force base in Little Rock to pursue a degree and begin my military career.

- - -

It was post-Vietnam, so the G.I. Bill was different than what my dad had. The Air Force paid for 75% of my tuition, and I was left to pay the remaining quarter, plus my books. All of the officers in charge of the base were college graduates—they had to be. Because I was one of the few pursuing a degree while stationed, the officers favored me, which afforded me special privileges. For example, they would be generous with EFD's (excuse from duty) if I had finals coming up and needed time off to study. They were counting on me becoming one of them. However, I was counting on getting out and making bank. Of course, I was not about to tell them that. I appreciated the flexibility that came with being one of their prospects.

My job in the service was working in the Titan II Intercontinental Ballistic Missile program. This particular program has been replaced with others since then. The U.S. has ICBMs hidden in plain sight all over the country. They are often in places you would not even think to look. The missile that I guarded was a good drive away from the base. To get there, you had to drive several miles off of main roads, then take a small road to a restricted area with armed guards and a barbed wire fence. We would then take an elevator down eight stories beneath the earth and protect a 180-foot tall rocket with a warhead on top.

In theory, if a nuclear war broke out, a massive 17,000-ton door would move back and the missile would deploy and swiftly kill a commie for Christ. That was the motto anyways. I guarded those missiles for the better part of 3 years. I was on for 24 hours and off for 48, which allowed me to study on my off days. The major downside of this particular job was that at times the alarm would go off at 2 a.m. I would have to wake up, get dressed, and drive 30 miles to inspect, only to find out a rabbit got under the fence and tripped the alarm. Technology has since come a long way.

My roommate worked in the same missile program. On one occasion, the alarm went off and it would not reset. When this would happen, we would have to go on-site and guard the spot until the alarm was fixed. It was an absolutely awful job. It basically meant you had to sit in the middle of nowhere in this compound for 10 to 14 hours by yourself. It was absolutely mind-numbing work.

Our friend group had a day planned at the lake when my roommate, Paul, got called in for this duty.

I was wearing him out, laughing, making fun, and rubbing it in. The razzing was harsh. I was immature and cocky, with no ability to read the room. The next day when he finally got off of a 14-hour shift, he came into our room, grabbed me by the neck, put me on the wall, and chewed me out. "Don't you ever do that to me again!" I felt ashamed and humiliated.

I walked out onto the balcony and thought, *Well, I deserved that. I've got to change.* Boot camp had worked some humility into me, but plenty of arrogance still remained. It was a paradigm-shifting moment for me because I realized not everyone thought my antics were funny. Sure, I was carrying a gun and guarding a 400 million dollar missile, but I was still a kid with plenty of room for growth.

If my college/military years did anything for me, they ground out a lot of the childishness that I had. If I had lept straight from high school to attempt to walk out a career, I would have been walking with a serious limp. The military gave me more responsibility than I was probably worthy of, which forced me to rise to the occasion. Sometimes giving people responsibility that's slightly beyond their reach will cause them to step up and stretch themselves into stewarding the responsibility well.

In the corporate world, I used to give my managers huge tasks that would sometimes be two levels above where they were. Occasionally, it would bite me on the butt, and they would do a full face plant. But more often than not, they would rise to the occasion. If we only lift what we are capable of comfortably carrying, we will never grow in capacity. It's by pushing the envelope that we *expand* our capacity. During these years, I was determined to expand my capacity in every way. On top of my 24-hour shifts every two days, I was taking four classes per week and studying whenever I had the chance. It was hard to be academically motivated in high school, knowing it didn't matter much in the long run. Not to mention my environment was anything but conducive to good grades. However, in college, I knew that what I did *counted*. I figured out that my performance would directly impact my ability to rake in money after I was discharged.

I didn't just act the part but dressed the part. I used to go to class in a suit and tie. I carried a briefcase and I took it as seriously as I could. I averaged a 3.8, which blew away my high school grades. I loved the grind. I did notice that not everyone in the military had ambitions, and that surprised me. I wanted wealth. I wanted to be something—but not everyone else did. Many of the others were fine with doing a couple of years in the service, getting out, and settling down with a decent job. As fine and dandy as that may have been, I was bent on *mega-wealth*.

- - -

"It's their building... they can do whatever they want with it!" Rent control in New York City was the hot debate at the time and I let my economics professor know where I stood. My mom was a dyed-in-the-wool Democrat, so liberal talking points were all I knew until I began studying economics in college, where I became a pro-free-market capitalist pig. The first election I ever voted in was in 1980 between Ronald Reagan and Jimmy Carter. I'll let you take your guess as to who I cast my ballot for. His last name started with an R and ended with -eagan.

While my professor agreed with me on rent control and other things, he wouldn't say so out loud. He was careful about voicing strong opinions, given his position. I learned a lot from him. He would take me golfing, engage in good conversation, and he taught me how to drink rusty nails—which were horrible. Majoring in economics and business administration was helpful, no doubt. But it was all just theory until I got out into the real world of business and got my nose bloodied.

My social life was flourishing in Arkansas, which provided relief from the monotony of work shifts and studying. Many of the wives of the officers were my classmates, so I found myself making friends with the very people who ran the base. I even made friends with the dean of the school and attended parties with that circle.

A year into school, some friends and I attended a Pat Benatar concert in Conway, Arkansas. I met a girl at the concert who I ended up dating during the remainder of my time in the military. Her family and I got along well, and they would even let me sleep on their couch rather than driving back to base when it was late. If I wasn't busy enough, I picked up some side work acting in commercials for places like Dillard's and doing some modeling as well. From the missile silo, my commercial would come on, and the guys would have a good time razzing me about it.

Having a life outside of base had several benefits, one being that I wasn't closely associated with some of the sketchier members of our flight. We once had a recall at 4 a.m. where a group of us were gathered and informed by some agents that the *Office of Special Investigation* had put a plant in our flight and had been working on a two-month-long sting. "Everyone in this room is fine, and we have not found any of you doing a controlled substance," they announced to us. "However, there are 80 other guys in the flight who are not so lucky."

They proceeded to arrest the 80 others, sending them to Fort Leavenworth jail before being dishonorably discharged. I obviously hadn't smoked pot with any of them, but I knew some of those guys. I thought, *Man. That could have been me! Their careers are over.* It was a wake-up call that if you play stupid games, you win stupid prizes.

One of the most consequential trips I had ever taken occurred during that time. November of 1979, to be exact. I remember the date because it was when the hostages were taken in Iran—a conflict that would go on for over a year. I went on leave to visit my uncle, who had recently moved to Dallas, Texas. I fell in love with the city instantly. The cars, the money, the women, the buildings—I was hooked. I thought, *These women are beautiful. They actually have ankles!* If I had any questions about where I would go after my time in the service, those questions were killed when I stepped foot in Texas. Dallas would be my destination. I knew it and I planned for it.

I had learned about human behavior in the police academy. I learned about money in my economics classes. I learned a lot about teamwork in basic. Yet I would soon learn a lot about the *real world* in Dallas. It was my city and still is.

As graduation approached, I mentioned leaving the military to my superiors. Wanting to hold onto a college grad, they asked me to stay on and become an officer. So I made them an offer.

"I'll stay if I can have $100,000 a year and a new Buick Riviera."

"We can't do that."

"Then I'm out."

And I was.

Sergeant then added, "It's hard to make a living out there, you know?" I accepted that challenge gladly. Without knowing it at the time, within two years I would have a new Cadillac and a six-figure income. Being a military officer has prestige, and I absolutely respect it. You can stay in for 20 years and leave with a full pension. But I would have gone crazy.

I began to seek out people in the service who knew people in Dallas. Someone knew a guy who owned a car dealership in Dallas. I went and interviewed and had an offer of $6.75 an hour to drive cars from lot to lot and essentially work as a gopher for the dealership. With a post-military job lined up, I began the formal process of being honorably discharged from the United States Air Force. I was given a huge envelope full of paperwork. I then had to visit several different offices at different times: the doctor, the discharge office, the payroll service office, and more. The entire ordeal took about a month to get through. I received my discharge orders after four years in the service.

My time serving exceeded my expectations, and I'm eternally grateful for it. There's a sense of pride that comes with it. I'm one of the few who is in favor of compulsory military service for two years for all able-bodied citizens. If everyone put on the uniform, our nation would look different—for the better. The disciplines, structure, and order wound up being instrumental for me and my future. With that said, when I left Arkansas in the summer of 1982, I was more than happy to be done. In fact, for a couple of years after discharge, I had nightmares that I was called back in because of a wartime situation.

In the service, when you're almost out, they refer to you as "short." The running joke was, "I'm so short I can walk under the door on my way out." I had saved up 60 days worth of vacation time so that I could leave two months before my official discharge date. I graduated with my degree from Arkansas State, and three weeks later, I shook my sergeant's hand, saluted him, got in my car, and never looked back. I was Dallas-bound.

CHAPTER FIVE

DALLAS

LITTLE ROCK WAS real. It was nice. But it wasn't *real nice.*
Dallas was. There was a "can do" spirit in Dallas—an entrepreneurial edge that felt like home. Comparing Dallas to my home city of Flint was like comparing Disney
World to Dante's Inferno. I rolled into the city in my giant
1970 green Monte Carlo. It was the length of a yacht and
boasted a gas mileage of 40 feet to the gallon. I stayed
with my uncle for a short spurt while I started my first
gig at Lonestar Cadillac Dealership. Since the *Post Vietnam Era Education Program* was still active, I decided to
take classes at the University of Texas night school. After
grinding at the dealership, I went to class at night.

Meanwhile, my brother Matt knew Flint was heading downhill, so he and a buddy moved to Dallas, too. He
scored a job at McDonald's and we three got an apartment
together. Even with three of us, we were all stretched to
make rent. We put an ad out and got a fourth roommate
to join us in our two-bedroom apartment. He was a Jew-

ish male dancer who ran a vending machine business on the side.

We were an eclectic, crowded, and broke bunch. I remember putting my life savings in the gas tank of my car at times—which was about 27 cents. Desperate to make it big, I asked my dad to help me get my feet wet in insurance. He set up an appointment for me with a State Farm district rep who was located in Dallas. "We would love to have you," he said. "To start an agency, you just need about $50,000 upfront. From there, you'll be set to earn a good $8,000 per year after that."

Are you kidding me? 50K just to get started!? He might as well have said it would cost 50 million. I didn't have anything, and I was not about to go into debt, only to starve in the years to come. At that time, I met a lady at college who was a banker. I complained to her about my job at the dealership. I had only been there for four months, but it was a mindless bore. "I'm financing this high-end clothing store in Dallas. I can get you a job there." I took her up on her offer and left Lonestar Cadillac. This store was run by an Armenian Jewish man named Martin, who was a genius. He was horrible, but a genius no less. He was selling deluxe Brioni suits that went for $3,000-$7,000 a pop.

Martin had a hot temper and very little tact, but he was brilliant when he needed to turn on his inner salesman. He was fluent in English, Hebrew, Mandarin, and who knows what else. Chinese businessmen would come into the store, he would pull out his Mandarin, and they would pull out their credit cards. It was not uncommon for a group of them to leave with $100,000 in purchases.

Three months into this job, I started noticing a particular group of guys who showed up to the store occasionally. They were all in their early-to-mid-thirties. I took note because they all would drive up in Ferraris and Lamborghinis. They would come in and drop tens of thousands at a time. Coming back from lunch one day, I noticed yet another luxury car in the parking lot—a Rolls-Royce. Sure enough, it was a young man from that group. As I walked in, he was buying four suits and ten ties, over $20,000 in product.

Eaten up by the mystery, I finally said to him, "What do you guys do?"

"We sell insurance."

"Do you guys work for State Farm?" My naiveté was showing. He laughed in my face.

"Why don't we have some drinks, and we'll talk about it."

My goal of being in the insurance business was coming together in front of my eyes. I thought it was just serendipity at the time, but many years later, I would believe otherwise. We went out to the club next door. The club scene was big at that time in Dallas. I was wined and dined with steaks and drinks. He said, "You know, I think you could join and sell insurance with us. You can make a ton of money and really help people in the process." I thought about it for a long and hard .0003 seconds. "Yes!"

I didn't sleep on the offer. Shortly after this initial meeting, I was in training. I took classes at night to learn the various insurance laws in Texas. This particular agency was selling life insurance and endowment plans, which was a totally new world to me. My boss, Martin, wanted me to stay at the clothing store. "Don't work for those guys. Stay with me," he'd say. He was a jerk about me leaving and laughably asked for an override on my sales when I started selling insurance. He might have spoken Mandarin and Hebrew, but he didn't speak McIntyre. I was gone.

It was about thirty days from the time I was offered an insurance gig until I was in the car, headed for Indiana with my new sales manager to learn how to sell this stuff. At the time, I didn't understand why we were going to Indiana. As a Michigan kid, Indiana was just the boring door you had to go through to get anywhere else in the country. But I was informed that Indiana had good leads and that deals were being closed there.

It was a great training ground for me. I watched my sales manager make several presentations in the houses of prospects over the course of four days. He skillfully handled objections and perfectly timed his rebuttals. In between appointments, he would go over all of the benefits of the contract with me and quiz me on the finer details. During his pitches, in the back of my mind, I thought to myself, *I can do this... and I can do it better.* I was a novice with unearned confidence and ambition coming out of my pores.

I was a sponge, soaking up as much as I could. I went back to Texas, passed my exam, picked up my insurance license, and was ready to go conquer the world. While I was licensed to sell insurance, I had no reliable transportation. This was a problem because I had hot leads four hundred miles away in a town called Wink. My old Monte Carlo was limping along, and I hardly trusted it to get me across town, let alone across west Texas. My uncle came in the clutch and rented a car for me to drive.

When I got to Wink, I checked into a hotel, practiced my presentation, and was out for the night. The next day, I went to my first appointments. After two days, I had made four presentations and wound up with a goose egg.

Zero sales. I knew the product, but I didn't know the people. If selling is an art, I was no Van Gogh from the start. I tapped my foot and bit my nails. I had very little money to my name, my hotel was $35 a night, and the rental car would slap me with a $200 bill. *Was this whole thing a mistake?*

Finally, during the last call on the third day, I hit pay dirt! I made a sale which I later learned would net me more than $1,000. While I knew it would happen if I stuck with it, I also couldn't believe that this sales thing was working! I made three more sales that week before I drove back to Dallas on cloud nine. The eight-hour drive felt like eight minutes.

- - -

Like a kid in a candy shop, I turned in my sales on Monday. The woman in accounting told me to come back after lunch to pick up my check. I obviously knew I had earned a commission on each premium I sold, but honestly had no idea how much, nor did I do the math.

I went to lunch in the brand-new Galleria Mall where our offices were located, and when I came back, I walked into the office, and the lady said in a thick Texas drawl, "Hey, honey, you did good your first week out of the chute. We couldn't verify funds on two of your sales, but I don't think you'll starve, sugar."

She handed me the check. I thanked her and headed for the elevators. When I got to my car, I wanted to evaluate my fortune or lack thereof. When I opened the envelope and pulled out the check, I had to do a double-take at the numbers. Payee: Michael McIntyre. Amount: $4,800.96. My heart skipped a beat. The statement also noted that when funds were verified from the other sales, another $1,600 would be coming. How do I describe what I felt while gazing at those numbers? Excitement is not a strong enough word. Excitement is what kids feel at a playground. Excitement is what women feel when they buy new shoes. I was not excited. I was *exhilarated*. I was *enamored*. It was an absolute, bonafide rush.

Now, you have to put all this into proper context. My previous W-2, which was for my last year in the Air Force, showed earnings of $5,400 for the *entire year*. And in just one week, I had made more than my entire previous year's earnings. Not only that, but $6,400 was more like $17,000 in today's money. I was hooked! I had found my calling. I then looked to see what bank the check was drawn off of. Conveniently, it was the bank right inside of the Galleria. So I went back in, cashed my check, stuffed all forty-eight of those crispy Benjamins in my front pocket, and walked back to the car feeling like I owned Texas.

I kept one foot in front of the other, hit the road often, and sold like a maniac. I didn't know it at the time, but I was apparently really good. It became real to me when we had our company Christmas party after my first year in the business. "The top salesman of the year is Michael McIntyre." The thrill of recognition hit me again as it did after the fundraiser at Holy Rosary. The difference this time is that, one, I was not selling light bulbs, and two, I did not win a $50 savings bond. Instead, I won a new car, a Rolex watch, and $5,000 cash.

As you can imagine, as my account balance went up, my motivation to continue college went down. I looked at my brother and had an idea. He was on the managerial fast track at McDonald's, but I figured he might be interested in a side gig. He looked a lot like me and could even pass *as* me in a big classroom. "Go to class for me, do all the assignments, and I'll pay you for it as long as you get a B or better."

He did that for about three months and got bored with it. So when he quit his job as a student-in-proxy, I dropped out of school. His two-week notice meant my academic career was being set down, never to be picked up again. I did not mind one iota because the money kept coming in. I could walk into a store and buy whatever I wanted. I was realizing a freedom financially that I had not known nor witnessed prior. Bringing in well over half a million a year (adjusted for inflation) meant it was time to break up the crowded party at the two-bedroom apartment. Matt and I went and got a nice apartment in the city.

The pay raise also meant it was time to ditch my oxidized chariot and buy something new. The dealership that had recently paid me $6.75 an hour was now selling me a brand new white on white, leather interior Cadillac Eldorado. Being a one-percenter at the ripe old age of 23 is a recipe for arrogance—and I had no shortage of that.

"I think *God* has something to do with this success of yours," my stepmother mentioned.

"Nope. It has all happened by my own hands," was my response. Pride came as easy as income in those days. Looking back, I told far too many people about the money I was making. People come out of the woodwork looking for loans, and I quickly learned that when you loan money, the borrower will resent you for it. When folks feel indebted to you, they avoid you. They feel awkward around you. No-strings-attached generosity, however, is a relational preservative. Of course, I was still learning all of these things and getting used to my new lifestyle.

Work at the agency was a lot like a big party. It was sort of like the Wolf of Wall Street life. We had several salespeople fueled by cocaine. I was blessed to see my older brother's example and *never* desired drugs because of it. I truly hated that scene and didn't touch it. Nevertheless, many partook and they would work for a week, make $5,000, and then take off for a month. I hated putting my feet up. I dreaded the weekends when I couldn't take appointments. Money was my drug. If I was not ambitiously chasing the next sale, I got restless. My manager loved me for this. I was making him a ton of money and was a top producer in the company.

At this point in the story, you might be thinking, *C'mon McIntyre... are you saying it was that easy? You just fall into a cushy job and attract all the money you can spend?* The answer is *no.* While I did have a knack for sales, that knack would not sustain me over the long haul. I had to become a quick-change artist, ready to improvise, adapt, and overcome as the marketplace was constantly shifting and my familiar tactics were becoming obsolete.

At one point, I remember feeling like I didn't know our product as well as I should. Our company had a conference for salespeople to brush up on the ins and outs of what we were peddling. I took copious notes and went back out on the road to share my knowledge. Weeks went by and I was not selling anything. It was a total face plant. I quickly realized I liked the feast better than the famine I was currently in. A more experienced salesman gave me an unforgettable insight: "Mike, you're taking your new, vast knowledge of the product and spewing it on the prospect all at once. Don't tell them *everything* about the product. You'll overwhelm them. Keep it light and stay relational. Give them the essentials of the product and keep it simple stupid!"

Armed with counsel, I hit the road, and the losing streak ended. I began to close as I implemented the new strategy. My prospects were no longer nodding off during my pitch. If you don't sell, you starve. But often, if you don't *shift*, you don't sell to begin with. This would be the first of many tweaks I would make over the course of a decades-long career in the business. Trial and error was my professor in those years. Experience was my mentor. I would soon undergo yet another shift as the owner of the agency was getting close to shutting down the business and moving on. I was not privy to the reasoning at the time, and I did not know the owner all that well. However, this would soon change as I became particularly interested in a young lady at the agency. That young lady happened to be his daughter.

CHAPTER SIX

FIRST COMES LOVE

I WAS IMMEDIATELY attracted to her. She was about 19, gorgeous, and a brunette—which was my flavor. She was working in the licensing office at the agency. Whenever I needed paperwork for an out-of-state sales call, I would frequent that department. After seeing Stacye, I had another reason to patronize that office. She was in from school at Texas Tech and filling a spot in her father's company. One of her friends introduced us in the hallway before she went out to play tennis on her lunch break. I still remember the tennis outfit she had on.

As much as I was drawn to her, there were some strikes against the situation. First, I had a girlfriend, and Stacye had a boyfriend at the time. However, the big kicker was the fact that her dad owned the agency. I did *not* want to date the boss's daughter, only for that to go south and my paycheck to be affected. I liked her, but potentially jeopardizing my job was not a thought that was floating in my orbit. That is, until a conversation with the girl who had introduced us.

"You know, Stacye wants to go out with you," she informed me.

Well, I wanted to go out with Stacye, too, so she put the bug in her ear. Shortly after, Stacye and I had lunch together, with her friend third-wheeling. The conversation flowed. She was more introverted than me, which I was drawn to. She was funny, kind, and smart. More lunches happened, and more conversations ensued. We talked and talked about anything and everything. When I would go out on the road, I would call her. I remember dialing her from a hotel in Nebraska and spending 3 hours on the phone with her. At checkout, my bill totaled $160.

"Who's the lucky girl?" the front desk clerk teased. I thought, *Oh boy. This is getting real.* We obviously ended the previous relationships we were in and quickly began to fall for each other. She caught me off guard one day when she said, "You have to talk to my dad if you want to go out with me."

I thought, *That's a deal killer. I'm not about to ruin this paycheck.* Around that time, we had a company conference where all of us employees were gathered together. There she said to me, "I told my dad that you want to talk to him."

"You did what?"

That got my heart pounding. *What was I supposed to say to the guy?* I called my dad, told him the situation, and asked for coaching.

"Look, tell him you're an upstanding citizen. Let him know you went to college, excelled in the Air Force, and that you will take care of his daughter."

I went in and scheduled an appointment with *the*

man. He made me wait in the lobby and sweat it for a solid 20 minutes. It was a huge, fancy office with marble everywhere. I just about blacked out every thirty seconds from nerves. Finally, he opened the door and waved me in. I sat down and frantically rattled off my resume in 3 seconds.

Fortunately, he didn't proceed to clean his revolver as I talked. He was gracious. As much as he was a charismatic tycoon, he was also an introvert with shy tendencies. It was disarming, which I needed. With his west Texas accent, he summarized our meeting by saying, "Look, there's a lot of cocaine and nonsense going around the office. I never want Stacye around that stuff. Be a gentleman and take care of her. Get her home every night at a decent hour. If you do that, we won't have an issue."

That was it. In a way, the meeting was superficial because he had already had me checked out, although I did not know it at the time. When he knew I was on the up and up, I had his blessing. That night, I took Stacye out for a nice dinner. She appreciated the fine dining. I ordered a $150 bottle of Dom Perignon, which gave my dad a heart attack when I told him about it later.

It became obvious that Stacye was the one. She had everything. Her look, her perspective, her personality—I was attracted to it all. I knew that I was fixing to spend my life in the insurance business as an entrepreneur, and it mattered *deeply* to me that she knew the pool I was swimming in. She had watched her dad do what I was doing and grasped the business. Her upbringing looked so much different than mine. She was sophisticated, and there was something enticing about that. She had traveled around Europe and had been schooled in the high life.

Not only was I drawn to our differences, but I was drawn to our commonality. Like me, she had been through a divorce in her childhood and knew what it was like to wrestle through the trauma of a broken home. We understood each other. As months went by, we were absolutely head over heels. It became obvious to me that I couldn't live without her.

- - -

Six months into dating Stacye, her father, Jack, closed the company. Understandably, he was looking to liquidate and slow down. I had spent half a year amassing cash by selling insurance plans. So the question became, *What's next? Can I hit this same level of success elsewhere?*

An opportunity presented itself in Arlington, just 20 minutes from Dallas, at Western Casualty Life Insurance. I would be in the same type of position—straight commission, a 1099-based insurance salesman with the only difference being, we were selling health insurance instead of life insurance. The company was owned by a gentleman named Richard Dale. There are some jobs that *bore* you and other jobs that *build* you. This was one that built me. Above anything else, I learned from Richard the ins and outs of how the business works. He was an eccentric Horned Frog TCU grad from a wealthy Fort Worth family. I observed him closely.

I learned how the entire process of the business functioned, from its infrastructure to its various departments. I gained a grasp on hiring and firing. I grew in my understanding of accounting, customer service, and day-to-day operations. I was beginning to see that my lane would someday expand beyond solopreneur salesman.

"Mikey, if you can bring people to sell under you, we'll put them on a contract and let you make some overrides." When Richard offered me this, I didn't realize how essential it would be to my story and development as a leader. I recruited my brother and stole him from the fast-food industry. Before I knew it, I had 7 or 8 people under me. Beyond my income from my own sales, I was earning $5,000 a week in overrides alone. This was around early 1985. I really worked at training them to be the best they could be. If they were excellent, it was good for them, good for me, good for the customer, and good for the agency.

I would often take them for ride-alongs when they were new. Before entering the home of a lead, I would advise, "When we go in there, look at me. Don't talk to the client. Not a word." As soon as they began to speak with the client, I would lose control of the pitch. On more than one occasion, I kicked my guys out and had them wait in the car until we were finished inside. Selling was not always rainbows and butterflies.

- - -

By December of 1984, I had been at Western Casualty for about six months and had been dating Stacye for a year. By then, she had met my family and I had met hers. Fortunately, that didn't scare us away from each other. In fact, my mother and siblings all fell in love with her. We would all get together, hang out, and have a good time. We were meshing and making it. It was time to go ring shopping.

Prior to buying the ring, we hadn't discussed marriage at all, but she had hinted that she was ready. It was a cool 50-degree night on December 22nd when I took her to a nice French restaurant for the special occasion. I was nervous! Despite always being myself around Stacye and being completely comfortable in her presence, there is something about proposing that makes a man shake. I popped the question from one knee and then heard that coveted three-letter response.

Stacye grew up Southern Baptist. In fact, there are more Southern Baptists in Texas than people in Texas. Most dogs in Dallas belong to a local congregation. Despite this, she always loved the Catholic Church. She thought it was romantic and reminisced about touring cathedrals in Europe. We began attending weekly Mass. While I didn't buy any of it, I appreciated the normalcy of the ritual. Six months later, we were married in that Catholic Church in June of 1985. My family all came in from Michigan and we had around 200 people at the wedding. The reception at the hotel ballroom was nice but awkward. My mom and dad were not getting along at all at that time, which was par for the course. Her parents were also not getting along at that time, again, par for the course. Despite all that, we were hitched, which was what mattered most.

We had saved up money and went to Maui for our honeymoon. I spent every dime I had on that trip. We spared no expense. After returning to Dallas, I had gotten a nice condo for us to start our lives in. I was 24 and she was 21. There are endless jokes made in marriage conferences and seminars about "the first year of marriage." It took me getting married to find out why. It was tumultuous at times!

Learning to live together was different. It took some time for us to learn each other and surmount immaturities. I would be on the road five days a week and come home. When I was home, I would want to go out and get a beer with my buddies, and she wanted time with me, which could cause sparks to fly. I eventually ascertained that my time was not my own and that my responsibility to Stacye outweighed my responsibility to anybody else. As with any newlyweds, we had to iron out our issues and learn to communicate.

During our first year of marriage, my father-in-law had a massive and unexpected heart attack. I remember racing to the Cardiac CCU unit with Stacye when we found out—we were both distraught. They were prepping him for open heart surgery when we showed up. When we got there, he opened his eyes, looked at me, and said, "Why aren't you out selling?" His humor was still very much present. I remember holding his puke bucket for him during recovery and seeing him in a more vulnerable place than I had before. Being out of the business turned out to be a blessing as it would take him some time to recover fully.

For our first year married, one area we didn't have much conflict in was money. It was coming in waves. I was overseeing my team while continuing to learn the insurance business and raking in commissions. I was the sales manager overseeing all of Texas, Louisiana, and Mississippi. Stacye would often join me on the road, and eventually, she said, "Why don't I set your appointments for you?" She began doing so and eventually booked my brother's appointments, as well. Involving her in the business was really healthy on all fronts. During those first few years, she bounced around to different gigs and stayed busy. However, she soon stepped into a role that far outweighed booking my meetings—*motherhood*.

CHAPTER SEVEN

STARTUP

AUSTRALIA, SWITZERLAND, ITALY, Hong Kong, Spain, and several other nations had all stamped our passports by the late 1980s. By this time, I had been recruited out of Western Casualty and began working for a similar company but a bigger one. It was a nationwide health insurance business where I was selling, managing a team, and most importantly—learning how to scale a large company. I observed the hierarchy structure of management and took notes on what growth looked like at that level. I knew they would come in handy later. I won lots of trips in that job, and Stacye and I became citizens of the world as we spent our mid-twenties bouncing around the continents.

Stacye wanted to get pregnant badly in those years. We were ready. We dabbled in self-help, visualizations, and some *new-agey* experiments. Stacye was into psychic practices and numerology in those years, too. That came to an end when I got a $900 phone bill from telephone psychics. There *was* one spiritual experiment that seemed to work out. She used to go to a charismatic church early in the morning and pray for a baby. Apparently, God gave her what she wanted because I got a phone call while I was on the road and heard those unforgettable words on the other end: "I'm pregnant!"

We had tried for a while, so I didn't even believe it at first. We were both absolutely thrilled! The nine-month dash was full of anticipation. Stacye began preparing the nest for our new arrival. She was focused on onesies and showers. I was focused on earning to pay for the kid's college. We had moved from the condo to a 3,700 square foot home with a pool in a great neighborhood. I continued working hard, and when I wasn't working, we continued our international travels. In fact, we traveled up until she was seven months pregnant.

Going to the hospital, we had no idea whether we were having a baby boy or girl. We were delighted to hear the words, "It's a girl!" We welcomed our firstborn, Brittany, into the world. It was emotional, beautiful, awe-inspiring, and wonderful through and through. She was perfect. I quickly gained an understanding of what unconditional love was. With the entry of this one tiny human being, I was *instantly* willing to lay down my life and give up everything for her. Parenthood is incredible. I also quickly felt the pressure of providing for this little one. Food, clothing, shelter, and education took on a new meaning. Watching Stacye thrive with the new baby painted her in a completely new light for me and my appreciation for her compounded.

By that time, my mother had moved to Dallas and was a happy new grandma. Jack generously brought a housekeeper in to help us out for the first few months.

That was a gateway drug. We have had domestic help ever since. Stacye's mom came in from Atlanta and stayed with us for a few weeks, which was a blessing. My dad and Betty really didn't involve themselves much in any of that—which was to be expected.

Being a parent shifted my perspective in ways that are beyond description. As any parent knows, every decision, action, and reaction is filtered through a new lens. There are added pressures but, more importantly, added *joys*. We were ebbing and flowing as a growing family. A sleeping baby became the new happy hour, as they say. Two years later, I became outnumbered three to one as our second daughter, Brianna, was born. Our hearts grew bigger yet again. Brianna was a colicky baby. She would wake up at 3 a.m.; I would change her, give her a bottle, and stay up with her until I had to leave for the office at 6 a.m. I would work 12 to 14 hours, squeeze in time for jogging and a workout, get to bed at 11 p.m., and do it again four hours later.

I was recently asked about that season of life, "How did you not burn out?" The answer is *because I loved it.* I felt like I was doing what I was meant to do. I loved my work, loved my routine, and loved being a dad. I'm certainly not saying that kind of schedule is a long-term prescription for everyone, but I was fueled by ambition and a newfound unconditional love for our babies.

On the weekends, we began attending Sunday services again. While I still wasn't any sort of born-again believer, I did feel comfortable with the church thing. It seemed to be a stabilizing force in our lives. It seemed to make sense that a stable American family would attend church together. A few years after our second daughter's arrival, we welcomed Brecca, our third, into the world.

That was 1998. David Frost said that having one child makes you a parent. Having more children makes you a referee.

Stacye and I loved the craziness of it all. Growing up in split homes, we had settled it from the start that our children would grow up in a stable nuclear family. It was by no means free from head butting and disputes, but we worked to develop a home culture that allowed for disputes with hugs and kisses at the end of the day. Our home life was transparent, vulnerable, open, and honest. As our girls got older and would hang out at other people's homes, they would come back shocked and say, "That family doesn't talk about anything with each other!" We worked at keeping an open-door policy as parents.

Each season of our kid's lives was enjoyable. We loved having dependent babies, ornery toddlers, curious kids, and moody teens. Every phase has highs and lows. We all navigate the tension of wanting our kids to stay small and not grow up too fast while at the same time we dive headlong into new seasons of growth and experience. We celebrate when they learn to walk, but we cry that they aren't tiny anymore. Every parent knows that tension.

Our girls ultimately became grounded, well-adjusted adults. They knew they grew up in affluence but made friends of all socio-economic backgrounds and didn't become haughty about it. I owe so much of their upbringing to Stacye's influence and care. What she did in the home was more important than what I did in the office. Stacye is the least pretentious person I know, who has every reason to actually be pretentious. I was pretentious but had no real reason to be.

In fact, one time, Stacye was doing some charity function in Dallas. She had a beautiful new Jaguar; however, as Jaguars go, it was in the shop. She had to be at Neiman's at 10 a.m. with no vehicle to get there. The housekeeper was at the house, so she borrowed her car. It was a 1989 Toyota rust bucket. Stacye's outfit cost more than the car. She didn't care. She wasn't prideful, haughty, or embarrassed. She pulled up front and center and valeted the thing. Me? I would have taken a cab and had the driver let me out half a mile from the event. Stacye is a true gem, always teaching our girls the *sunshine method.* Meaning the sun shines on all people, not just a select few. As a result, everyone deserves kindness at all times. Our children grew up in privilege but maintained friends of all socio-economic backgrounds. Had I had the same roots as them, there's no way I would have wound up as grounded as they are.

There is so much more to be said about parenting and marriage that perhaps we will save for another book, but I will say this: it's worth the fight. Having seen the firsthand effects of brokenness, we wanted better for our children. An intact family unit not only made sense in the home but made sense in the boardroom. A wholesome family life lends itself to corporate growth and career excellence. I didn't have to worry about divisions in the home dragging down my entrepreneurial success. When my business life hit low points, which I will soon relate, I could count on stability at home to keep me grounded.

- - -

I had spent ten years like a sponge in the insurance world and it was time for me to be rung out. The insight I had gathered working in other firms would soon be released as I started my own. It was 1990, and Jack was now fully recovered from his heart attack. Being a serial entrepreneur, he was ready for a new venture. I had some savings in the bank and American Express in my wallet. I was always a fan of unsecured debt when leveraging a new startup. If things go south, American Express just puts ketchup on that debt and eats it, and I don't have to lose my house.

I was 30, a new dad, and high on ambition. I was never one to chase every single shiny new opportunity willy-nilly, but rather to wait for the *good* opportunities. This seemed like my chance to do something new and become a business owner at the same time. Plus, I would be doing it with the help of a master mentor who believed in me and gave me the confidence I needed. The premise of our company was to offer insurance within the estate planning model. We saw a mass wave of US citizens hitting retirement age over the next decade and wanted to target them. Plus, the laws for inheritance and taxation were favorable to the insurance business at that time. We saw the opportunity and decided to start it. We spent enormous time and money putting the firm together.

We took a small office that I already had leased and expanded it. Where I lacked confidence in the early days, Jack encouraged me and gave me the necessary vision. He let me do what I felt to do and that helped validate me. He gave me a lot of rope to make mistakes, which I hung myself with a few times. After months of planning and building infrastructure, we were ready to launch the company in 1991. We recruited and trained employees from the area. The massive company I had worked in went out of business, meaning 4,000 salespeople were out of a job and looking for a lifeboat. The market was hot for recruiting good salespeople.

When we did our first mailing, we borrowed $17,000 from the equity in a car we owned. We did a 100,000 piece direct mail campaign. It took four weeks before we saw anything. Then, we did. We pulled a 4% return rate on those 100,000 ads. It was unheard of at the time.

I'll never forget our first sale. I was so pumped. It was a true paradigm shift! Everything looked different after that. I woke up the next morning, and on the way to work, it was like somebody had given me a brand-new pair of glasses. The sale validated what we felt was true—that this could work. From scratch, we had built something and generated revenue. Now we weren't making a profit yet, but we were bringing in revenue. Our biggest issue was being undercapitalized. We were operating solely on American Express cards and whatever cash we had coming in. Once we put a hodgepodge staff together, we started training them to go out and sell the product.

Jack and I shared a little office with a conference table that we sat at, me at one end, Jack at the other. Sitting across from him day in and day out, I learned much that I have been able to apply to my career. He was an absolute master with people. Despite butting heads with him at times, I knew I was being taught by a consummate professional and that was invaluable to me. He was like a tough dad. At times, my ego would be bruised and I felt he was picking on me, but at the end of the day he always had my best interest in mind. I knew he cared about me. People would say, "Michael, Jack brags on you all the time." This always surprised me because he wouldn't say those things to me directly. But having his approval, covertly or overtly, was a confidence boost I greatly enjoyed.

On February 19, 1992, everything changed—for myself, my family, and for the company. We received a phone call that Jack had another heart attack. It was different this time. Everything about it felt different. There would be no recovery. There would be no surgery. He died at 53 years old. It hit us like a freight train. We broke down. We wiped away tears. We broke down more. Stacye was a daddy's girl—the loss was devastating for her. We cried together often. The grief was not something I had been through prior. In fact, for 18 months, I felt as though there was a black cloud over me nonstop. I had lost my mentor and my father-in-law.

On the business front, things were not looking bright either. The company was flailing. Despite a working model, litigation issues began to cripple my enterprise. It was a sinking ship. Without Jack's guidance, I had to make hard choices on my own. Just two weeks after his funeral, I got a phone call from someone at a national newspaper asking for comment on a "sting" operation. I was completely caught off guard. The paper had secretly taped one of our sales representatives during a presentation.

To my dismay, I discovered that the rep made misleading comments and answered questions that should have been referred to a lawyer. While this was obviously fireable and *completely* against policy and practice, it was cause for accusation to fly and negative press to spread about our company. I immediately called our team of attorneys. When the article hit, it was not favorable, to say the least. The next two weeks were madness. We were on CSPAN and Newsweek, and the Associated Press were calling for interviews. Lawsuits were being filed against the organization alleging misrepresentation and the unauthorized practice of law. The lawsuits were politically motivated. Our company had made several powerful enemies.

Our business model was perfectly legal yet novel. The *newness* of it ticked off some 800-pound gorillas who didn't want us playing in their sandbox. Essentially, we would hire attorneys in several different states through a service called *prepaid legal*. We formulated a deal that was good for everyone. We would sell premiums and introduce the estate planning option to a client, and then refer that client to our partner attorneys. It had just become legal for attorneys to advertise, so we quickly jumped on the opportunity.

When attorneys in these states saw our model, they felt like their toes were being stepped on, so they accused us of practicing law without a license. We, of course, were not. However, the one out-of-line salesman became the rule, not the exception in their minds. It was all extremely political and nasty. Lots of attorneys, several state bar associations, and third party interests were all coming after us.

Today, the same practice we had is commonplace. Firms like LegalZoom and IncFile use a similar planning and referral method, and they have done quite well. At the time, however, the practice was so new that it lit a fire under those who were threatened by it. When forging a new industry, there is going to be plenty of blood spilled in the early days of battle. This was no exception. I was in crisis mode.

My attorney informed me that Maine was about to file a suit with us; he helped me get in touch with the former attorney general in Maine, a man named David. On the phone, he said, "Michael, if you look at the television, the attorney general and the governor are getting ready to hold a press conference. They are talking about your organization." I hired him, sent him a check for a retainer, and he flew down to Dallas on Easter Sunday. I picked Dave up at the airport and took him to the hotel. The next day, he came to the office and we started damage control. I desperately needed coaching on how to deal with these crisis situations.

The first thing he did was advise us and our attorney to go to Oklahoma, where our vendor's headquarters were located. So we chartered a small plane, flew to Oklahoma, and had a meeting with them. After our meeting, which lasted about an hour, we were walking to lunch on the small town's main street when David pulled me aside and said, "Mike, you need a friend. Your vendor and their attorneys are not your friends!" Upon returning to Dallas, David made a few phone calls, one of which resulted in an appointment the next morning with one of the biggest law firms in the city. He then explained to me that there had been a huge conflict of interest, which made matters worse. Apparently, the law firm that represented our company also represented our vendors.

It was a major business blunder, and I had to try to correct it. Thank God for David's voice as an objective third party in the situation. My hope was that it wasn't too late to steer us clear of a collision with bankruptcy. *What would Jack do right now?* I was really missing him. I desperately wanted to know what he thought. David filled the gap momentarily, and I knew I could trust his advice, but it wasn't the same.

Going to bed that night, I felt optimistic that the next day would be better. *We'll get to the bottom of this tomorrow, for sure,* I thought. I had no idea what was coming next. We went to downtown Dallas the next day, met with our new counsel, retained them, and began to turn the situation around, or were trying anyway. Over the course of the next few days, we had several meetings. During that time, I was introduced to an attorney named Jeff. He was a little younger than me but very smart and likable.

He called me a week later and explained that he had arranged a meeting with the firm's senior partner for the following day. The next day, I got there and was shown to the big conference room on the top floor of the building. My attorney and the senior partner came in, and the senior partner did all the talking about all the varying problems we had. Then he finally got to the meat of the conversation and said, "Michael, what you need to do is file bankruptcy." *Oh, my God!* I thought. It hit me like a ton of bricks.

There I was, thirty-one years old. I knew that I owed some money and had lawsuits coming in, but I couldn't help but think, *How can I sit here and file bankruptcy, not pay the vendors, not pay my agents, and still have integrity?* I knew it was a small town, a small world, and if we wanted to survive long-term in the business, bankruptcy was not the right thing for us to do. I looked at our options. Our attorney said, "Michael, pay off your house as soon as you can. You might get sued and lose your cash, but they won't be able to take your home." That sounded wise, so we threw our cash at clearing the mortgage. Any remaining money we had, we used to clean up the mess we were in.

When it rains, it pours. Over the next several weeks, it just got worse. Not only was the loss of Jack still fresh, but I found myself bursting into tears just driving down the street. I was in panic most of the time. In the end, I stuck to my convictions and chose not to file bankruptcy. Instead, Jeff and I fought and settled, one by one, every claim brought against the company. It took over eight months and all of the money I had left, but we did it.

Ultimately we stopped selling and closed the company. It was a devastating shift going from running an exciting, innovative, fast-growing company, working side-by-side with my father-in-law... to Jack being dead, the company being closed, and spending months fighting legal battles. It was a very bleak time. With a wife and two young children to support, I had no time to sit around feeling sorry for myself. Wound-licking does not pay well.

If the military had taught me anything, it was that you have to adapt quickly to your environment. One moment you're sound asleep dreaming about the beach and the next moment, you're running full throttle in the middle of the night with a sergeant screaming your ear off. In business, one moment I was running a budding enterprise, and the next moment I was cashless and unemployed. What do you do? You deal with it. You get up, rub some dirt on your cuts, and keep going.

Ultimately, I had two options: I could get back into sales and make a living at another agency, or I could embrace the headache, take the risk, and start another company. My rational internal voice said, "Settle down in sales at a reliable firm." My inner entrepreneur roared, "Begin again!"

I listened to the latter.

CHAPTER EIGHT

ENTERPRISE

THE PLAN: MARKET to the masses so we could dine with the classes. Most agencies that dealt in retirement planning and annuities focused on people with millions in retirement accounts. While gorilla clients like that are exciting, they wouldn't be our bread and butter. I reasoned that there were a lot more people with $200,000 estates than $2 million estates, and we would go after them. We didn't need a big cash cow when we could have thousands of cash calves.

I was 31 when I launched this insurance marketing firm. While our products were not novel, our *system* was. Many think they have to reinvent the wheel or innovate a new product to make it in business. However, if you can innovate the *system* of facilitating that sale, you can do just as well. Consider how many people have built businesses that depend completely on electricity, for example. These businesses didn't have to *invent* electricity but simply build systems around it. In fact, a British physicist named Faraday was a leader in the early discovery of electricity. When asked, "What use is electricity?" by the queen, he famously responded, "What use is a baby?"

In other words, it's not about the invention's *current state* but the invention's *potential* in the future. The future possibilities of a baby are endless—and so it was with electricity. We saw our products, insurance and annuities, as *potential* and built a method around them to exploit that potential.

The insurance world was and is very competitive. It's a red ocean, blood-in-the-water business. Our "blue ocean" strategy was to separate ourselves from the shark tank and do something that hadn't been done, which was to pair insurance sales with attorney-facilitated estate planning. No insurance marketing firm had done estate planning with attorneys up until that point.

While the firm would have a similar model as my previous company, we made a few key changes. First, we removed ourselves from big associations that brought too much attention and risk. Second, we would contract attorneys state by state who would work directly to help our clients with what we could not. Contracting attorneys was a lot easier than hiring sales reps. Most attorneys cannot hit water jumping out of a boat when it comes to marketing. They generally aren't sales-oriented. But their services in estate planning were valuable, and we needed them to play a key role in helping our clients.

Beyond that, I had great legal counsel. With the sale of any sort of financial instrument, especially in the senior market, you are going to be a target for litigation. To minimize this, we overkilled it with disclosures and a proper legal framework. We did everything through the lens of the federal trade commission and went through proper regulatory agencies in each state we operated in. Any Fortune 500 company that exists has hundreds of consent decrees—they all get hit with lawsuits. Even the best-paved lanes have potholes. We were no exception, but we wanted to make sure litigation would not squash us. It was essentially a more intentional and organized pipeline than we had before.

Perhaps above all else, I *believed* in our products. You can sell anything if you just need to make a living, but selling a product that you actually believe in brings a different level of fulfillment. Single premium annuities were a fantastic product for us. For example, if our client was 70, had a 10-year horizon, and $300,000 in the stock market, it was easy to show them that a market crash could cause a massive dip in their balance that they may not have time to recover from. Volatility was the risk we specialized in mitigating. Often our clients would liquidate their shares and place the money in an annuity.

This allowed their retirement to grow tax-deferred in an account with rates that were 2-4% higher than what banks were paying. The other plus was that if they needed to access some funds, they could withdraw 10% annually without penalty. The major selling point to those with descendants was that annuities bypass probate upon the death of the owner. The funds just go straight to the beneficiaries—hassle-free. For these reasons, we found it to be a terrific financial instrument, and so did our clients.

It only made sense that as we discussed big financial moves, the topic of insurance and deeper estate planning with one of our attorneys would come up. Selling intangible insurance products really allowed us to build a story and an aura around these products as we pitched them to our prospects. It wasn't sexy. We weren't selling yachts to billionaires, but we were selling shelter and safety to cherished and revered people, many of whom had been overlooked by the market because they weren't in the millionaire class.

My first hire was my brother, who came back to work for me. For the first three months, it was just him and me. We went out and *sold, sold, sold.* Our clients thanked us, and we thanked them. That kind of mutual gratitude is the exchange of value that good businesses are built on. The cash flow was good. I had made a couple hundred thousand dollars in the first three months. I poured all of it back into the business to get this thing off the ground. We *perfected* the system and built a scalable prototype. Yet, I knew that the next level would not come unless I built a team before I built a mass clientele.

- - -

Before I detail how I built the team at our company, let me give you some context. Early in my career, when I was selling health insurance, I used company-provided leads. Every Monday, I would go to the office, turn in my sales, and collect a check and a new deck of leads. I would then get on the phone and set up my appointments for the next day. Some leads were great, and some were duds.

After making as many appointments as I could, I would travel and "run my appointments." During the day, I stopped at any payphone I could find to set appointments for the next day. To those born after Y2K, a payphone is a communication device with no apps that eats your quarters and lets you talk to prospects by pressing a dirty piece of plastic against your face.

It was really hard at times. However, in those days, that was what worked, and as long as you had the self-confidence to deal with plenty of rejection, you had a good chance of succeeding. It did not take long for me to realize that setting my appointments *and* running those appointments was too much. As I mentioned in an earlier chapter, Stacye had the idea to set my appointments for me.

"Are you sure you can do this? You haven't ever sold anything."

"I have been listening to you for the past year and a half. I know the script by heart!" she said. The next day, Stacye took my leads while I went out to run my appointments. Two things took place: I found I was able to *completely* focus on making sales. And two, I made *more* sales because I was in a better mood, not having to think about appointment-setting.

When my day was done, I returned to Stacye, who, to my delight, had scheduled four appointments for the next day. Over time my sales doubled, we had more time, and the divide-and-conquer method was super successful. Not only that, but my brother Matt began paying her for scheduling, too.

It's simple: if you need help, get help. If you think you might be able to use some help, get help. If you think you can do it all yourself, get help. Sure, you might be able to do everything in your firm, but at what cost? Learn to leverage your talent to its fullest potential—meaning you delegate the things that don't excite you and focus on the things that do. Otherwise, you will eventually *dread* what you refuse to *delegate*. Obviously, there are seasons where you have to grind and get by. But the long-term play is to maximize your strengths and hire out your weaknesses.

In my case, I didn't have to hire out this weakness because my wife had stepped up and carried the load.

Unfortunately, after three months of this arrangement, my prima donna began to show. I had had a tough week on the road and the lack of sales was getting to me. Some of the leads I was meeting with had recently had surgeries or preexisting conditions, which totally stopped us from getting them a policy. All of the appointments felt like a waste of time. I called Stacye and forgot who I was speaking with—a big mistake.

She answered the phone, "Hey, how was your day?"

"Not worth ****!"

"What's the matter?"

"These appointments you're setting aren't worth a ****! Why did you set them? You know we can't sell them if they had bypass surgery last year!"

"Hey, don't yell at me! The leads are difficult this week; I'm working as hard as I can. In fact, *why don't you just set your own appointments from now on!*"

I groveled and tried to backtrack, but it was too late. She was not on payroll nor on the clock. She was just lovingly making my life easier, and I had the nerve to be a jerk about it. Ashamed, I called her that night with a sincere apology. I then asked, "What should I say to Matt about his appointments?"

"I'm going to keep setting his appointments. He never complains. Besides, he pays me every week."

Ouch.

Her help had allowed me to reach new places of success, and I blew it. Seeing the remaining need, I quickly took an ad out in the paper for an appointment-setter and found one, a lady named Babbette. She was a trip. She cost me five hundred dollars per week. It was a valuable lesson: don't complain to the people doing you favors.

Beyond that, I learned something that would shape the way I structured my business: keep appointment setting and sales *separate*. In doing so, you will empower salespeople to be salespeople and support people to be support people. Babbette went on to take care of my paperwork and even helped me build a call center later on that would do nothing but set appointments. When it was time to recruit agents a few months after starting the company, I drew from these valuable lessons. I knew that sales folks want to feel like rockstars. So we treated them that way.

I knew that to grow our revenue, we needed salespeople. Yet to effectively onboard salespeople, we needed a mousetrap that made the job easy-peasy. The goal was to treat them like Bono, meaning they just had to show up and perform. We took care of the lights, sound, and stage and sold the tickets. My role shifted. I was no longer selling our product but selling new recruits on the merits of working for our company.

I was advised by a mentor, "Listen, McIntyre, no matter what happens in your week, no matter how much business you're writing... the last thing you need to do *every single week* on Friday is get your ad in the paper to bring in new recruits." I became aware of the one-third rule. At any given time, one-third of our recruits were leaving, one-third were staying, and one-third were onboarding.

I developed a system called RTM^2, which stood for recruit, train, motivate, and manage. We spent 1.4 million annually on training our people. We flew them in from all over the country. They would tour our corporate offices and go about in-depth training with our national marketing director. These training sessions occurred almost weekly.

Long before *Undercover Boss* became a hit series, I occasionally infiltrated our training events. This was the pre-social media stone age when no one knew what the boss looked like. I would put on a fake name tag and walk through the process with a group of new recruits as though I were one of them. I loved hearing what was happening and figuring out who was there to meet girls and who was there to actually advance their career. On the last day of training, I would take the name tag off and introduce myself to the crew. They would promptly go into shock. We recruited over 20,000 agents in my career. The methods of recruiting and training eventually became the building block for the training organization I would one day start. Yet for now, I was sticking like glue to my mentor's advice: *get your ad in the paper every Friday.*

We advertised "free leads" in our sales ads. Most of our people who came in to sell had spent their final $5,000 on a lead system that didn't work and came to us broke. The notion of "free leads" was like a hot meal to a beggar. Beyond that, they absolutely fell in love with the thought of not having to schedule their own appointments. We made it easy for them to come on board and begin earning six figures fast. We brought in mass numbers of leads through direct mail, had full-time schedulers setting appointments, and had the salespeople out executing on those appointments.

We didn't need 10,000 agents to scale our company. In fact, we took 100 agents and did more than brokers with 5,000 agents because our guys were *free to focus* on the close, not the scheduling and paperwork. It was the basic principles of *the division of labor* applied to our area of focus.

I loved watching people go from broke to making tons of money. Writing checks with a comma was a big deal for me. So many of our agents were misfits with overdrawn accounts and cars in repossession. When they showed up to work for us, they began to thrive and turn their lives around. That end of managing people was every bit as satisfying as helping the clients themselves. It did not take me long to realize that becoming successful was sweet, but setting up others for success was even sweeter. Christ's golden rule was turning out to be true for me. Father Rob would have been proud.

When an agent came in who was broke and had a marriage that was on the rocks, we would often call their spouse to come in and pick up their first paycheck. "Go home and present this check to your husband." We wanted to see marriages healed because finances were in order. Allowing both parties in the marriage to experience increase created mending moments. At the time, I had no idea how prophetic these small assignments were.

Day to day, I was hands-on hiring, recruiting, and training. When I was looking to hire key positions, I would often take people out to lunch and observe how they treated wait staff. If they were terrible to the waiter, I could count on them being terrible to their co-workers and subordinates. Shifting from selling to leading was a natural fit. I began forecasting and taking care of big-picture items. The 14-hour days felt like bliss. I loved what I was doing. I was hooked on the rigor of creating something from nothing.

Within just one year, in 1993, we were selling 1 million dollars a week in premiums. It put us in the top 20%

of all agencies nationwide. Not to mention, we were doing those numbers with only about eight sales reps. We were a lean and mean machine with no sign of stopping. In fact, around that time, one of our top salespeople got word that his mother-in-law had died and he had to move to Kentucky. He was inheriting a farm and needed to work out those details.

I hated to lose the guy.

"Why don't I recruit an attorney in Kentucky for you to work with, and you can sell there? You can set up our Kentucky office!"

He was game.

I ran an ad in the area and got well over a dozen responses from local lawyers. We flew out, set up at a hotel, and interviewed 14 attorneys until finding a couple of them that we liked. We began doing mailings, getting schedulers, and our new Kentucky sales manager began producing. We realized that we had just developed a model that could be reproduced in *any state.* Voilà. We were no longer a local business. We were a nationwide agency with our sights set on pioneering offices in Tennessee, Georgia, Alabama, California, and eventually 34 other states. The gettin' was good, and we were certainly gettin' it.

CHAPTER NINE

IMPOSTER SYNDROME

"YOU'RE THE LAST to be paid... but you'll be the *most* paid," Hal advised me. That line stuck with me. Being last in line was frustrating, but being in line for the biggest check was exciting. I lived in that queue for a year. It was in early 1994, twelve months into launching the company, that my frustrations came to a head. I was paying my bills and keeping the lights on at home, but meanwhile pouring every bit of extra money I had back into the business. My overflow was reinvested in direct-mail leads and payroll. We had five office staff and a dozen reps. The administrative costs were high.

Everyone around me was making a lot of money. The salesmen were raking in three to five thousand dollars a week. The admin staff was paid generously. The lease was not cheap. Meanwhile, the founder was pulling out just enough cash to buy groceries and diapers. Running payroll was like pulling teeth. *When will I start seeing this payoff?* I went to my mentor.

Hal Altschuler was a veteran in the business. I had met him earlier in my career when he ran an agency of his own. A Jewish man with marketplace wisdom and a great sense of humor, I gleaned from his insight and he quickly became a mentor. We shared a middle name and both of us had spent time in the service. He really brought me alongside him and helped me make my first million dollars years prior. He had no problem with me making $50,000 in a week under him, but if I bought a $4,000 suit he would have a heart attack.

During World War II, he flew 33 bombing missions over Germany and got two Purple Hearts. He flew seriously damaged aircraft from neutral countries to England, risking his life for his country. He left the Air Force with the captain rank. He ended up going to law school and practicing for a while before getting into the insurance business. Once he did, he went big, setting up agencies all over the U.S. and Canada. He was a true *mensch*[1]. Hal took me by the hand when my father-in-law died and helped me navigate hard times. He loved to see me succeed. He was a charmer. Stacye loved him, and I did, too. Occasionally, he would hear out my ramblings and frustrations.

"Everyone that works for me is making more than me! This isn't a charity. Where's mine?" I complained. That's when he advised me with the eternal words that began this chapter. With his counsel in my holster, I went back to work armed with confidence. In the few months that followed, I kept at it. Then, *the levy broke.* Money came in... and not in a small way. I did not start earning six figures. I started making seven figures—and that number would not drop in the years that followed. I had

---

[1] A Yiddish word, meaning a person of integrity and honor.

sown bucketfuls of money into the company and was now reaping wheelbarrows of it. Hal was right.

What accounted for the increase? At that time, people in the United States had estates that were getting bigger than they had been in ages past. Bringing estate planning into a new light and setting up plans to avoid unnecessary estate tax and probate was in high demand. We were on the cutting edge of this boom. I saw the opportunity and steered the ship accordingly. If people didn't like the direction, they were free to get off and swim. My leadership style was pretty straightforward: I paid people *a lot* and demanded *a lot*. I was unreasonable at times. I knew that. But I also knew that unreasonable people *get stuff done.*

I was heavily involved with every end of the business for the first five years. An ample amount of my time was committed to growing and motivating that team. Reid Hoffman once said, "No matter how brilliant your strategy, if you're playing a solo game, you'll always lose out to a team." While I respect solopreneurs, I knew that my vision required many, many hands on deck. I worked closely with the salespeople and developed contests and hosted conventions. Being a salesman myself, I was keen on how to get results from this group.

I worked with CEOs of insurance companies and continued to promote our distribution capabilities for their products. I hired MBAs to handle the books and accounting. I hired attorneys to provide in-house general counsel. I oversaw the call center, HR, and the C-Suite team. I often traveled to set up and oversee our new offices that were popping up around the country.

Looking back, I had my hands in too many areas in the early years. If I could offer advice to a new CEO or founder, I would say, *Bring in professional management and trust them.* Let them do what they need to do. It's difficult letting a new person babysit your newborn, but at a certain point, you have to take a fat salary, get some perks, run a division that you love to run, and let the others do the rest.

As the money multiplied, I started to enjoy the fruits of my labor and traveled more with the family. I eased off a bit. However, I didn't sit back, put up my feet, and light my cigars with $5 bills. I was still a workhorse, but I would take much-needed vacations and I wasn't breathing down my staff's necks all the time—which I'm sure they appreciated.

- - -

It has been said that, "The value of a company is the sum of the problems you solve."[2] We must have been valued pretty high, because we weren't short on problems to solve. Dogs don't chase parked cars. We were moving, which attracted some yappy mongrels. If a 75-year-old client had $500,000 in an A.G. Edwards account, after meeting with us they might liquidate their holdings and stash it in an annuity—protecting them and theirs. This ticked off the stockbroker who would challenge us for having "misrepresented the product" to a protected class of senior citizens. In reality, he took issue with his commissions being vaporized—not the legality of our practice.

In fact, the federal government wanted to make annuities a financial security rather than an insurance product. The SEC saw a ripe product and worked to pull

---

2 Daniel Ek

it under their umbrella. This meant certain death for countless agents who didn't have a series 6 and 7 license, which would be required (among other things) to sell a security. It would be like showing up at a Ford dealership and telling the owner that his salespeople needed to be licensed space shuttle salesmen in order to push F-150s.

I wound up being sued by the government. It was a huge deal in our industry. I spent almost a million dollars in attorney fees and spent nearly three years thwarting off distractions and litigation. The result? We won. In a summary judgment, the case was settled. The appellate court threw it out and annuities remained an insurance product.

When news broke that "McIntyre beat back the SEC and stood up for the insurance world," I figured I would *pass the hat*. I had been the canary in a coal mine on behalf of our industry. Considering the revenue that we had saved other companies, I figured they would rush to chip in $100,000 apiece to the legal fund.

After all, we saved countless jobs and saved the insurance industry 300-400 million dollars per year. Instead of contributions, I received many thank yous and firm handshakes. People appreciated the win—but not enough to pull out a checkbook. My shoulder gained a chip or two after that.

Beyond litigation, in the insurance business, you sometimes attract scalawags who are less than integrous. If you can pass 4th grade and fog a mirror, you can get a license to sell insurance. That doesn't mean you will be good at it, but it does mean that the barrier to entry does not resemble the Harvard admissions department. As a result, unscrupulous people came through our agency at times. With our rate of growth, you couldn't help it. Occasionally a rogue agent would present in a misleading way and we would deal with them accordingly. A hearty "see ya never" was quickly uttered after we put out the fire.

The biggest disruption, however, occurred four years into the company's story. My brother was working as our national sales director at the time. I loved having him work for me. He didn't always love having me to work under. That's essentially what it all came down to. He really wanted to quit at one point and even called me while I was in Cancun on vacation to turn in his notice. I spent a few days on the phone with him begging him to stay. In hindsight, I should have let him quit. "To everything there is a season,"[3] and when we artificially extend those seasons, they often turn sour. He reluctantly stayed on and then quit for real about six months later.

He was leaving behind over half a million dollars per year, but understandably, wanted his own agency and set out to build it. During that falling out, Hal sat us down for a meeting to do some mediation, to no avail. He left and took some of our top salesmen with him. I got mad and sued him. He sued me back. It was ugly. It split the family up for about five years. The suits were eventually dropped in mediation after hashing it out for months. This book is not a case study on family drama, so I'll spare you the gory details. I will say there was plenty of regret on both sides. Fortunately, we would later reconcile. *Unfortunately*, we would split again after that.

People would like to think that business looks like Mister Rogers' Neighborhood all the time, but it often looks more like Jerry Springer—especially when going into business with family. Pursuing a venture with family is an easy thing to *start* but a hard thing to *sustain*. It's

---

3 Ecclesiastes 3:1

an easy thing to jump into because it's the path of least resistance. You love them and they love you. You picture making beaucoup bucks, taking extravagant vacations, and riding into the entrepreneurial sunset together. In reality, resentment, triggers, disproportionate effort, and personality clashes can tank the relationship fast.

I tell people who go into any sort of legal business partnership (which I've always avoided) that they need to have their divorce papers drawn up before the marriage begins. This means you should know exactly how the inevitable split will go down before you get started. Have a buy/sell agreement and an exit strategy in place ahead of time so that you can have a drama-free separation with no hard feelings.

While my brother and I didn't have any sort of a legal business partnership, his leaving the company should have been thought through before I ever onboarded him. Lesson learned. It was a dark time. During that season, I had great people to lean on. Stacye was instrumental, supportive, and always ebbed and flowed with the highs and lows of the industry. Many times, it seemed like she understood parts of the business even more than I did. With the risk of sounding like a Hallmark card, the decades have demonstrated that we were *a match made in heaven*—and I mean that literally. She has been a grounding force in so many ways.

On the business end, I also had support. Tony was an attorney who worked as part of my in-house counsel and became a great friend. We golfed, laughed, worked, and talked. I had an excellent, smart CFO and a top-notch assistant, Jan, who remains a good friend to this day. They all acted as pillars in their own way. A good network can make bitter times better.

- - -

After Matt left, I went through five different national sales directors. I had unrealistic expectations for the job. I thought everyone should be as driven as me. They weren't. I used myself as the standard to measure up to, as opposed to objective standards that everyone could agree on. The founder is generally not the best or most realistic measuring stick because nobody cares about the company as much as the pioneer of it.

As our offices were popping up around the country, travel became heavy. I was on the road all the time. I chartered a couple private jets and loved it. It was a gateway drug. I had to have one. No long lines at the airport. No cancellations. No screaming babies. It was more than luxury lust, though. Logistically, I could check in on a few different offices around the country and be home for dinner with the family. At the time, we were selling 200 million in premiums a year with 25 million in gross revenue annually. I could swing it. I came across a Learjet 25 that was for sale in Binghamton, New York.

The owner came into money trouble and could no longer pay the bill. It was repossessed and the guy still owed $225,000 on it. So I flew to New York and plunked down $225K and brought the plane back to Dallas. After putting another $400,000 into maintenance and upgrades, she was ready to fly. We kept the plane at an FBO (fixed-based operation), which was an airfield called *Million Air* just north of Dallas. I hired two full-time pilots and became accustomed to doing business at thirty-two-thousand feet. My pilots had great discretion. Where I was, who I was meeting with, and the nature of my business calls needed to be kept low profile. "I heard the boss is meeting with an investor who is buying the company," was not the type of rumor I needed circulating. That plane treated me well and kept me mobile for the next two years.

The industry had been good to me. My entry-level sales gig had turned into a CEO position at a major company, and my oxidized Monte Carlo had turned into a private jet... and it only took a decade to become an overnight success, as they say. I was 34, making huge money; I was married to my dream girl; we had healthy kids; and I had a plane, a boat, and 400 employees around the country. While the business definitely presented challenges and problems, the formula worked, and because I loved what I did, the money felt so easy to come by. I loved the success—but it was tainted.

For starters, it didn't *actually* fulfill me. Deep down, I was not *truly* content. Sure, I was having fun. I had nice things. It's nice to have nice things. But there was an intangible lack in my heart. Resolving this would not come for another eight years. Second, the success came with a side effect: *paranoia*. If you are living paycheck to paycheck, you might look at the numbers I've thrown out in this book and think, *Paranoia!? I would sleep like a baby with that kind of cash cushion!* The truth is, it's not always that simple. Bigger money means bigger problems.

I began to deal with something that's commonly referred to as *imposter syndrome.* To put it broadly, imposter syndrome *is a fear of being found out as a fake* because you lack the ability, skill, or credentials. Now, I didn't lack the ability or skill, and I doubted neither. However, I did fear being found out as unqualified because I was a young gun from Flint with just an associate's degree from Arkansas State running a 400 person national firm. I had no Ivy

League degree—yet some of my employees did. I did not come from money or impressive academia. In fact, many of my employees had MBAs from the best schools; meanwhile, their boss did not. I would pay them $200,000 per year while I was making significantly more. On paper, they were qualified. Often, they were smarter. Yet, I was the one calling the shots and bringing in the money.

Who was I to run an operation like this? I would walk into the office and see people whom I didn't know or recognize. The thing was growing beyond comprehension. *Will people find out that I'm not some genius tycoon? How will they respond when they see who I really am?* I fought these thoughts for a while. Without guidance, I solved the mind glitch by becoming cold. I would rub my salary in the faces of team members who were better educated than me. I masked my paranoia by razzing others. "You went to *which* school? And *I'm* the one writing *your* check!?" I was pretty well versed in snobbery.

My bottom line was growing, but so was my awareness that I could not do it all on my own. I was money-addicted and hard. I busied myself with business and worried myself with work. I was headed for an existential collision but could not see it at the time. Stacye was fairly invested in her church life, but that was all hocus-pocus. I would show up on Sundays, cut big checks, and proceed to let the sermons run off of me like water off a duck's back. The scandals in the Catholic Church made me question my roots. If there was a God, He sure didn't care about what was happening down here. My mother turned to New Age trends, and I dabbled, but nothing ever stuck. As far as I was concerned, I didn't need any of these crutches because crutches were for injured people. I wasn't injured. I was thriving, or so I told myself.

CHAPTER TEN

GROWTH

I EMPTIED THE glass of vodka. It was not my first of the night. Mellow enough to comfortably take the stage, but sober enough to give a coherent speech, I walked to the podium. We had around 500 people in the crowd. It was most of our employee base and their spouses. As someone who now speaks regularly as part of my profession, I'm embarrassed that I needed liquid courage to take the mic back then—but it's where I was. I was self-conscious and a little intimidated. I hadn't spoken publicly much since sharing my recruiting technique with 1,500 other salesmen several years prior. I got a standing ovation then. *Time to see if I can do the same now with my own company.*

I proceeded to welcome, thank, and encourage our employee base. We gave out awards and plaques, celebrated successes, and championed our people. It was a hit. These company conventions began just a couple of years after we started and continued for the duration of

our existence. The gatherings provided much-needed camaraderie and motivation. With offices around the country in 40 states, it was easy for employees to feel discon-
nected from one another and from the central vision of
our home base.

We flew everyone in from all over the country, and we
gathered in Dallas, where we wined and dined them first
class. It was important to me that our employees knew
that we had deep wallets and a willingness to take care
of them. We were not a fly-by-night, makeshift operation.
*We will take care of you if you take care of us, and if you take
care of us, we will take care of you.* We had a circular trust
with our team.

Stacye was heavily involved in the planning and ex-
ecution of these conventions. She knew the price of being married to a traveling salesman, so we gave shopping
money to the wives and scheduled manis and pedis for
them as their hearts desired. They were picked up and
escorted in limousines to the Galleria, where they were
met with champagne and fine dining in the evening.

Besides this annual event, we did an exotic company
trip every two years with the executive team and some
of the top salesmen. Early in my CEO career, I became
a big proponent of retreats. It was a chance to get everyone out of their element to let their hair down and enjoy
themselves, without work-related pressure. We would
eat, drink, and meet.

Taking 150 people to places like Monte Carlo, France,
Rome, Cabo San Lucas, and Vegas was not cheap, but it
was well worth it. At the end of the getaway, we would
end up with a bill for $750K but, more importantly, a mo-
tivated and refreshed group of leaders. Retreats were not
just a carrot we dangled in front of our employees, but

they were the fuel we put in their tank before they went out and slayed giants.

Outside of the retreats, our company culture was all business. We wore suits and *casual Fridays* didn't exist. I reasoned that if you dressed casual, you *thought* casual, and if you *thought* casual, you were a soon-to-be *casualty*. We spared no expense with our corporate offices. At $20,000 per month, our 15,000 square-foot lease was on the fourth floor overlooking north and south Dallas. When we took it over, I had all of the walls torn down and had glass walls installed throughout the interior. It was an impressive space, complete with executive quarters and a deluxe boardroom. We were within walking distance of some of the best restaurants in Dallas. Even if traffic was heavy, it was just a 5-minute commute from our house.

We were selling a ton of insurance at the time. There's no other way to say it. We were moving $400 million per year in premiums and were in the top 2% of all insurance agencies in the nation. I had not sold in years, but I missed the simplicity of that life. Back then, I had no marketing decisions to make nor payroll to oversee. Now, instead of selling, I was raising up sellers. In fact, if I was forced to work on the company for just five hours per week, it would have been in recruiting. It was the priority.

When I was recruiting salespeople or promoting managers, I always had my eyes peeled for people who had experienced *real struggle*. If someone was two years sober, I was immediately drawn to them. They knew battle. They knew how to win under pressure. They could use sandpaper as a blanket and be fine. It's called *grit*. If someone was still standing after tragedy and had beat the odds, I favored them. I could trust them at the plate in the bottom of the ninth. I had seen the Ivy League grads with rich parents and no adversity who folded like a cheap tent when trouble came. I wanted the people who had scars to prove it. We raised up the best leaders we could and poured into them. It built a loyalty within the ranks that was truly invaluable.

As a result of that investment, I took it very hard when people quit. I saw it as a personal rejection. I was not just competing for clients but competing for strong employees—a market that can be just as competitive. When they would leave, it stung. At the same time, when people quit, I did not chase after them. When they were off the boat, I pulled away from the dock. Our industry was a competitive red ocean. I didn't have time to lick wounds.

Looking back, it is clear what made good employees good employees: *they were self-starters.* They went for it. They hustled. We might have butted heads at times or disagreed over decisions, but they were loyal and gave it their all, no matter what. They craved hard work. They lived for the grind. They didn't want their hand to be held, but at the same time, they could easily correct course if called out.

I also noticed another quality in good employees: *they were not victims.* They were not a bag of excuses disguised as an employee. They owned their mistakes. I always hated excuses and even coined the phrase *excuses are seducers to mediocrity* after hearing my fair share of them. If someone came in late and gave a BS excuse, I was prone to firing them on the spot. "I'm sorry. I'm late. I messed up," was a phrase met with mercy, whereas excuses were met with none.

At some point, our salespeople developed a reputation as complainers. They say if you give a salesperson

$100K in cash, he will complain that you gave it to him in 100s and not smaller denominations. At that time, I was spending 10 million per year setting appointments for the sales department. They seemed ungrateful. If they walked into an appointment and the person didn't have a check written for the premium on a golden platter, they complained about the quality of the appointment.

So I brought them all to Vegas—40 or 50 of them. I rallied the troops and said, "It's a great day today. Effective *immediately,* we are shutting down the call center. We will give you more money, and you can set your own appointments from this point forward." I've never seen a room of people backpedal so quickly. "Nooo, we love having the appointments set for us. You don't have to change anything…" I let them sit and sweat for a full day until they saw the light.

After they walked the plank, I brought them back in and said, "Listen, I'll keep setting these appointments, but if I hear you complain one more time, I'll never set another appointment again. Are we clear?" My language was likely a little more colorful than that… neon even. From that day forward, they never complained, and production went up dramatically.

I was hard-nosed. I would have a vision, so to speak, and see the direction the company should take as if watching a movie. I saw it plain as day. I would then convey that direction to the team, and if it didn't catch on, I had no grace for anyone. I was demanding, but I was also demanding of myself. It was not a "This standard is for *thee* but not for *me*" situation. I was not chomping cigars and making demands of people, but was requiring the best from myself first and then the team.

I wanted to make our people wealthy. That was it.

As you can imagine, my upbringing and military background lent themselves to this style of management. I was not interested in garnering love and admiration.

We are in an age where retail investors can buy and sell securities from apps in just seconds. Kids in their teens and twenties are trading, when that used to be reserved for old men with a Rolodex on their desks and suspenders. The conversation often comes up, "What's your take on investing and debt?" During this period of the late 90s, my business was not leveraged at all. I had zero debt and liked it that way.

I am, however, a fan of unsecured debt when pioneering a business. If you have an Amex with a $50,000 limit, it can be a great fulcrum to expand your business. I have often told young entrepreneurs that the worst thing they could have when starting is *money*. That's right; I said it: *money is the enemy of a startup.* Why? Money makes you lazy. If you have a $10,000 cushion, throw it in an annuity so you can't touch it and get your business off the ground on plastic. It's a self-inflicted boot-in-the-backside.

If you fund new business opportunities with a HELOC, that's a different story. If you don't see an ROI, you can lose your house and hurt your family. The same thing is true when borrowing money from friends or family. Has it worked out for some? Sure. Is it a best practice? Absolutely not. There's too much emotion, stress, and pressure involved. If things go south, you want a clean exit, so structure your debt accordingly.

Debt should never be a willy-nilly decision. Measure twice and cut once. You need to know your potential upside before you *ever* borrow. A small business loan officer will require a business plan in writing before he or she funds you. Because MasterCard does not require this, some entrepreneurs get lazy. They fail to make a plan and fail to run the numbers. Their ROI goal is just wishful thinking, not a bonafide calculation. Numbers that haven't been crunched ahead of time have a way of growing teeth and biting you in the backside. Test your ideas with a mastermind group. Find a brutally honest coach or mentor and ask them to sink your battleship and call your baby ugly. If your idea survives the scrutiny, you may have something worth funding. At the end of the day, I would rather have a bruised ego than a bruised bank account.

In the late 90s, my investment strategy was pretty straightforward. I was putting $200,000 per month in the bank and diversifying my investments. I was, for the most part, a Benjamin Graham-style *value investor*. I bought municipal bonds for tax reasons and bought shares in companies that I believed in. I held Coca-Cola, Ford, IBM, and other companies with strong fundamentals. I watched the markets pretty closely and read the Wall Street Journal and Barrons. Being a lifelong Disney fan, I owned $750,000 in their stock. When Disney dropped to $15 per share after 9/11, I sold and lost a significant part of my investment. That stock is now worth over $150. I haven't done the math and don't plan to. Lesson learned: the only people who get hurt on the roller coaster are the people who jump off.

Anyone with a wallet and a little intuition was jumping on the dot com bandwagon back then. To my chagrin, I thought the internet was a big joke at first. I was a slow adopter.

"Why don't you have email?"

"I don't care about that stuff... besides, I've got a pager, man!" was my response.

It was 1998.

Some of my staff had been using Excel and computers, but the company was still relying on call centers and direct mail, so the dot com boom didn't alter our business like it did others. When I eventually did get an email address, I thought it was the greatest thing in the world. I was late to the game but glad to be in the stadium. In fact, the only reason I have social media and an awareness of tech today is thanks to my daughters.

When people look back at the dot com era, they feel like it was just a gold rush of opportunity, and every start-up you threw a dollar at became Microsoft or eBay. I never wear those rose-colored glasses because I remember the frequent failures. I lost money on a few. A gentleman on my street owned a company called PageNet. He was third-generation money. He convinced me it would be a smash hit. I put $200,000 into it, and it tanked and went to zero. Another buddy who invested in it with me resolved, "I'll never trust third-generation money again!" I lost money on other dot com investments during that time, but it was the price you had to pay to get a spot at the table. If you said *no,* they would eventually stop asking.

I did not understand the technology, and because of that, I didn't enjoy investing in things I didn't understand. I had web developers who would promise to build us a website for $50K, and six months later, it was still not finished and we were out $120K. It left a bad taste in my mouth. However, I found opportunities elsewhere. I had an attorney friend, Pat, who was a frickin' genius and a conservative investor. He got me into some great deals.

He called me up with his thick southern drawl. "A developer in Plano has got money for houses, but no money for the land. I'm puttin' in $250K. You know me. If this goes south, I'll bawl for the rest of my life. You in?"

I was in.

The deal returned 90% in 90 days. My $250,000 became almost half a million. That's $225,000 in profit in three months, for one reason: *I had a seat at the table.*

- - -

Money got bigger, and so did the house. We sold the home we had enjoyed throughout the 90s and bought a one-acre lot in Dallas for half a million dollars. It was expensive dirt—even more so now with appreciation. Ross Perot lived three houses down. In fact, four billionaires lived in just a one-mile stretch on that street. By some miracle, I had gone from a dead-end street in Michigan to billionaire row in Dallas. We built a really big abode on our lot. We had Range Rovers, Jaguars, Mercedes. We had *stuff*. Interestingly enough, the *stuff* would only make me happy for a *moment*.

By opening up my books, so to speak, and letting you peek into the lifestyle and the numbers I was dealing in, I know I run the risk of sounding boastful. It could come across like a brag book when, in fact, it's anything but that. Why? Because *despite* the successes, I was empty. This is not the story of a hero, but the story of a man searching for one. As a new millennium was approaching, I still hadn't found him. By and large, I was unfulfilled.

What is a *lack* of fulfillment? It's a slow death without actually dying. It's like drinking from a golden goblet, but the only thing in the cup is saltwater. Shiny objects might distract you from your thirst for a little while, but your soul's needs can't be ignored long term. It's a gaping wound that can be stitched shut with a good fiscal quarter, only to burst back open on a downturn.

The grind was starting to outweigh the gold and the glory. Every morning, my assistant drafted out my non-stop schedule for the day and had it waiting for me at my desk. I took the company's temperature as I looked at the sales reports. I was filled in on what kind of recruiting was done. I was briefed on how much money went into the bank at noon. I would send national voicemails out to the offices around the country. We had a way to verify who checked their voicemail, and if a manager did not—heads rolled.

I knew that if you don't *inspect* what you *expect,* you shouldn't expect anything at all. Twice a month, I would get on my plane to do a surprise visit to a couple of offices. I had a phone on my jet and would send out a voicemail to all of our offices. It went something like this:

"Happy Monday morning to you! This is Michael McIntyre coming to you live from 40,000 feet. I'm coming to visit one of you... make sure you're ready." *Click.* I could hear 40 guys around the country throwing up in their wastebaskets. I wanted to open the file drawers at any branch in the country and see the same stuff in their file cabinet as we had at the headquarters. My aim was for the company to look like a franchise with consistency *everywhere.* I grilled the managers, "Who is your number one salesperson? Who needs training? Who needs correction? Who needs to be loved on?" I wanted to affirm, correct, train, and motivate during those surprise visits. They were a really healthy way to keep my finger on the pulse.

I was also dealing with CEOs and other companies constantly. I was on the phone like a telemarketer and traveling like a politician on a campaign. My lunches were generally business meetings, and I found myself stepping away from Disney vacations with the kids to take phone calls. Our national office count fluctuated between 35 and 46 offices in operation at any given time. It was *a lot* of work. Every. Single. Day. Just recalling it makes me tired.

I remember being in my thirties and seeing men in their 60s who were struggling with the job and not cutting it. I would have to let them go. It was painful beyond words. It was not totally cutthroat—I gave plenty of second chances, but part of being the boss is making hard choices and having excruciatingly dreadful conversations. Having a grown man cry in your office, begging to keep his job, does not make for a good day at work. Some of those meetings still haunt me. The truth is, nobody sees that stuff. They see the cars and the jets, but they don't see the tough calls. They don't see that you are *always on* and cannot just casually unplug after you drive home at 5.

I would attempt to unwind with trips to Vegas, where I'd play great golf courses and live the life of a high roller. I jogged six days a week, which I still do. We toured the world, and I fell in love with Italy. Yet, I would come back from vacation even more tired than when I left. I needed a shift. That's when we were approached by General Electric about a potential acquisition. GE was looking to acquire us and take us under their insurance wing.

We hired Ernst and Young to come into the firm and do a total appraisal. I hated that process. They were all MBA accountants, and having them scrutinize every part of my baby felt brutal. I didn't like them poking around, but it was necessary for the evaluation. My plan was to sell, kick my feet up, and see how fat I could get for 90 days. After that, I would probably do what serial entrepreneurs do and start something else.

GE, which was led by Jack Welch at the time, put a heavy 8-figure offer on the table. We countered with a bigger sum. They came back with an attempt to meet us in the middle, and the deal eventually fell apart. Realistically, they would have employed me for two years after the acquisition as part of the purchase, and I had no interest in that. Both parties mutually left the deal on the table for a handful of reasons. I was disappointed and felt like I had wasted lots of money on the audit. I didn't get the sabbatical that I needed, so I shifted again. That's business: being a quick-change artist. Entrepreneurship is a life of transition, so don't get stuck in paralysis analysis.

- - -

I set my sights on acquiring another company—my brother's. By then, we had reconciled and were on good terms. We would have drinks together and shoot the breeze on occasion. I heard through the grapevine that his firm was not growing at the rate he wanted it to. The next time we connected, I planted the seed.

"Why don't we merge our companies?"

His response was coy... but I got him thinking about it.

Six weeks later, he called me. "Hey man, you got me all excited about this deal, then you went MIA. Let's talk through this."

I met with Tony, my attorney, and we started to make

plans. There was a lot of apprehension, especially among the wives, because of how ugly the split was the first time through. Nobody wanted a repeat of the season one drama. His top management and lawyers got together with my top management and lawyers and secretly planned out the arrangement for a four-month period. The agreement was that I would give him a good seven-figure amount for his company, I would take sole ownership, and he and his 100 employees would keep their positions and, in most cases, receive promotions in my company. My brother would become the national marketing director, and his top management would move to oversee all areas of the company. After four months of negotiation and planning, we had a deal.

We went to Fiji for my 40th birthday—it was October of 2000. We were on a tiny island with 14 huts and a handful of couples. The deal was set up and we had a closing date ready. I waited in line to use the one single landline on the island. I remember talking to Matt, and we were both full of anticipation for the deal. I thought to myself; I *should have done this years ago.* I missed him. I needed a running buddy. Business is a battle, and I had scars to prove it. I was also grieving the lost time we had experienced from the falling out. Both of us were full of expectations.

After I returned, we brought everyone from both companies together to a hotel ballroom and made a massive announcement. It was a big move but made sense. I was really burned out and was thrilled to let them run things. Looking back, I made some mistakes. I was so ready to do the deal that I overlooked some things that I shouldn't have. Eagerness is an expert at blinding you to red flags.

The first year of the merger was incredible. We *tripled*

our business in twelve months. We were moving 18 million dollars a week in product. I had visions of grandeur—the McIntyre brothers on the cover of Fortune magazine. We toyed with the idea of going public—but our revenue was just on the cusp of satisfying IPO[1] requirements. Meanwhile, I was able to take on a more *hands-off* role. My relationship with Matt was great. We would hang out at each other's pools, go to our kids' birthday parties, sit around, drink beer, and talk about life and business. It was good again.

The kids were growing up, our family traveled often, and I was involved in the Young Presidents' Organization. I really developed an admiration for CEOs like Michael Eisner and Jack Welch at that time. They took companies that were hurting and nursed them to health and caused great growth. They then knew how to back up and trust the team to do the work. I was trying to follow suit.

---

1 Initial Public Offering

CHAPTER ELEVEN

NEW TERRITORY

TO NO ONE'S surprise, Stacye was always more spiritually connected than me, but I liked the ritual and the normalcy of attending weekly services. *The American Dream* was an incomplete puzzle without finding the church piece, so we looked. We dabbled in traditional, denominational, and nondenominational gatherings. We tried lots of flavors.

We wound up finding a small Methodist church and liked it. The way I saw it, churches had three types of people involved: the pray-ers, the players, and the pay-ers. The pray-ers did the praying, the players worked as the professional clergy, and the payers gave the money. I wanted to be a payer for two reasons. First, recognition. I remember taking the pastor and her husband out to dinner and giving them a $10,000 check to have the church organ fixed. I was purely after acknowledgment, not benevolence. Second, it was a way for me to keep the church off my back. If I was a giver, it would keep them from prodding around in my life.

I remember the church was once looking for folks to pledge money for a fundraiser. I don't remember the details, but I thought, *I guess I'll give fifty thousand or so.* So I did.

The next week, a man approached me. "Hey, we noticed the amount you pledged... did you mean to do that?"

"Listen, I don't come here to count money... will you leave me alone?"

He was courteous, just trying to verify that it was not a mistake. I was cold, annoyed that I was being questioned about money in church. I eventually got invited to the inner circle and attended the private Bible study. I figured out pretty quickly that it was all the big business guys in attendance. It further confirmed to me that the church was a corrupt money-grab.

The Bible studies were not great. Despite my Catholic school background, I had no clue where to find anything in the Bible. For all I knew, the book of Job was about how to find employment, and King James was the guy who wrote it. After four weeks of attending those private studies, I stopped going. I was disillusioned by the whole church thing and just did not see a place for it. Sex scandals in the Catholic Church had me thinking that *if* there was a higher power, he was no *holy power.* I would attend on Sundays with the family still, but I was certainly not about to become the *born-again* type.

In fact, in those years, I once turned down a 10 million dollar deal because a guy wanted to pray in my office. It's embarrassing to recall, but this book is my honest recollection, not my honorable resume. I had known the gentleman from 15 years prior in the insurance world, and he was down on his luck. He owned a client list that was valuable, and we knew we could profit from it. In fact, we wagered that we could bring 10 million in revenue from the list. He would have gotten a piece of the action in the form of a finder's fee. Sitting with my executives, talking through the possibility with him, he made a suggestion: "Can we pray about this?"

I was calloused. I was cold.

"Absolutely not. Get out of my office and take the list with you."

I was harsh. I was heartless. He walked out.

"Can you believe that guy? The nerve..." My C-suite team nodded in agreement.

I was self-made and self-sufficient—prayer opposed that notion, so I opposed *it*.

- - -

At the turn of the new millennium, the country had plenty going on. The Y2K scare had fizzled out, the dot com bubble burst, and George W. Bush was elected president. We had not been to an inauguration up until that point, so we decided to fly to D.C. to attend. I did not have tickets, so I called up the Pentagon Ritz Carlton. I talked to the concierge and asked to be hooked up. He said, "I need $10,000—and it needs to be cash." That worked for me.

I showed up, handed him an envelope, and we were given a badge. We dressed up and made our way to the national mall. As usual, it was a bitterly cold day in January. I really wanted to have good seats and be as close to the front as possible. With my ego, I wanted to be the guy to hold the Bible the POTUS was sworn in on. We ended up being about 40 yards from the podium. I said to

Stacye, "I wonder if we got good seats?" I realized we were sitting pretty when I turned around and saw nothing but a sea of people from the row behind me to the Lincoln Memorial over two miles away. We went to the dinners and balls that followed, wined and dined, and had a true blast at our nation's capital.

Something else happened around that time: I got the itch for another plane—a bigger one this time. The Lear-jet had a tiny bathroom, and I couldn't stand up fully in the cabin. First-world problems? You bet. I wanted the Cessna Citation III. It seated 13 people, you could stand up in it, it could fly 2,800 miles nonstop, plus it was out-fitted with a TV and *full* private restroom. It was a *big* step up. They went for $7 million, but I found one for $5.3 and felt like I got a deal. I then put $200,000 into upgrading the interior and was ready for the sky, or so I thought.

I didn't know it at the time, but this plane was known as a *hangar queen*—meaning she spent a lot of time in re-pair. The plane needed a phase 5 inspection and would need to fly to Raytheon in San Antonio to get it done.

"This type of inspection is sophisticated. It's going to be $150 grand," they told me. *No problem.*

Meanwhile, Stacye's brother was engaged, and their wedding was set to happen soon in San Diego. I figured there would be plenty of time for the inspection and we would be able to fly several people out there on the jet. They called me from Raytheon. "Hey Mike, the plane is going to need this repair. It will be another $150 thousand."

A week later, the phone rings. "I hate to do this, Mike, but you can't fly without *this* and *that* part being replaced, too. It's going to be another $200 thousand."

That happened a few more times until our total bill

was $750,000. *Yikes.* It was painful but had to be done. The *just-slap-some-duct-tape-on-it* mentality doesn't fly in this situation—literally. The plane was scheduled to be completed and returned to us on Friday, and we were set to fly out for San Diego on Saturday. On Friday afternoon, I got a call from our pilot, who was on the ground waiting for the plane to land in Dallas.

"Hey, your plane just got in from San Antonio. They're circling the airfield. The crew is foaming the runway."[1]

"Why are they foaming the runway?"

"The landing gear won't open and they may have to crash land."

My heart sank.

He continued, "Even if landing gear pops out and all is well, the FAA is going to ground this plane for 2 weeks for more inspections."

As it turned out, nothing was wrong with the plane. A simple indicator light had failed and they landed safely, thank God. The plane landed, but my irritation took off. I had to go buy plane tickets for everyone to fly to California.

With three first class seats left, I put my wife, mother, and sister up there. Me and the kids flew coach. It was an odd picture: I had just spent $750,000 to repair my $5 million airplane, and here I was sitting in the last row in the middle seat, in coach on a commercial airline. I griped and moaned the whole way, to put it mildly. It was a humbling experience.

Eventually the plane was up-and-running and we flew it around the country for several years. In fact, we flew into New York City in late summer of 2001. A com-

---

1 Foaming the runway means spraying fire suppressant chemicals all over the landing strip.

pany I was representing was IPOing, so we went to New York for the opening bell. We flew out of Manhattan on September 9, 2001. We did not know how drastically the skyline was about to change.

The tragedy of losing nearly 3,000 Americans on 9/11 was followed by a mental health plummet and an increase in suicides. Rumors of wars had many in a panic. Not to mention over 2.5 million jobs were lost, impacting families all over the country.[1] Lady Liberty was hurting. The event clobbered our business for a solid six months—we lost millions. The reason was simple: nobody was buying annuities or making big decisions. The markets froze. Our clients did not want to sell during the correction and take losses. Our pitch was not palatable because of the global instability.

It took us a full year to recover, but we bounced back and pressed on. The markets normalized and we began profiting again. Even when we invaded Iraq in 2003 and uncertainty was in the air, the company continued to increase and the markets grew until 2007.

My hangar queen was getting the best of me, though. It was becoming more of a headache than it was worth. It was a maintenance hog. The repairs were constant. I had tried to sell it after 9/11 but nobody wanted to buy a private jet in 2002. Finally in 2004, I got a call from my accountant.

"Look, we have a buyer for the plane. Let's just ask what's left on the note and get out of it."

That sounded great to me. I just wanted to be done with the hassle.

"By the way, who is buying it?"

"A guy you probably don't know, but his name is Jerry Falwell."

I didn't know much about him. I just thought he was an overweight blowhard who started a college. I didn't care who he was. I was just glad he would take the hangar queen off my hands.

I quipped, "Great. I hope there is a God because they are going to need one with this airplane."

The deal was done—I sold my jet to Jerry Falwell and never wanted another. Phantom tax came back and bit me. The only good financial benefit of owning a jet happens on April 15th. You can write that thing down like crazy and save on taxes with depreciation. My accountants had written down my jet to a value of $1.7 million. When I sold it for $3.2, I owed capital gains on $1.5 million. The hangar queen screwed me one last time. I now advise people who are coming into wealth to just charter planes when they need to fly. The jets boosted my ego but not much else.

- - -

Just a couple years after the acquisition with my brother, we split again. We were both more mature about it this time. The split occurred for similar reasons as the first. I did not want the company to be a two-headed monster. Over time, his people went back to him as he set out on his own again and my people stayed with me. Ultimately, it was like the acquisition never happened. He came into my office some months later and apologized. We both reconciled and made up. It wasn't nearly as brutal as the first instance, but I was on my own again.

I was caught between two desires. Part of me wanted out of the business completely. I had been in the industry for over two decades and I was tired. The other part of me

wanted to sink my teeth into growth and keep expanding. I had acquired a small benefits company and started
doing TV commercials for it. I ended up spending hundreds of thousands on TV ads that completely bombed.
Just because you make money doing one thing does not
mean you'll have automatic success in another. The core
of the company still had great revenue, but the side ven-
tures were not succeeding.

In a last ditch effort, I tried to pivot. The annuity business had been good but the wave was getting smaller.
The business model was becoming more of a corporate
agency with salaried reps rather than being built on hun-
gry, straight commission salespeople who raked in huge
numbers. I could see a new trend: single premium life insurance. It was a better alternative and I had discovered
a way to move annuities into single premium whole life
so that clients could take cash out for trips and expenses
while still bypassing probate. There were trillions of dollars in the annuity market that could all be moved to this
better vehicle—the market was endless.

There was a small company in Texas offering the
product, and I wanted to sell it for them. I picked up the
CEO in Waco and flew him to Possum Kingdom Lake,
where I and a doctor friend took him out on my sea ray
boat. I really wanted to get the deal done. I loved their
product and knew it was the direction the industry was
headed. However, I scared him. He was intimidated by
the dollar amount that I could produce for them. His
company just did not have the reserves nor capacity to
handle the growth. We were capable of writing hundreds
of millions in premiums. We were accustomed to selling
annuities for American Equity, run by Dave Noble, who
was a mentor and friend. I could mention 10 million dol-

lars to Dave, and he reacted the same as if I had said 10 dollars.

Dave was providing our company with $250,000 in lead allowance monthly—non-recourse. A lot of people in the industry didn't like that I was getting $6 million a year on lead gen money, but Dave Noble did. Why? Because I was putting $40 million in premiums per month in his checking account. You do the math.

This CEO, however, was not Dave Noble and was not comfortable with my numbers. I talked too big, too fast, failing to read the room. The deal dissolved, and so did my desire to continue running the company. It was sort of the nail in the coffin. I wasted no time planning my exit. Looking back, selling off my company in 2007 was like safely parachuting out of an airplane that was going down. Could I have picked myself up after the 2008 crash and pressed ahead with the business? Sure, but at what cost?

I could not quite stomach the thought of moving ahead with day-to-day regulatory issues, hiring and replacing managers, and grinding it out for the foreseeable future. I was tired of pushing the rock uphill. The juice was no longer worth the squeeze. I should have sold in 2000, but my ego kept me in it. The split with Matt extended things further, but I did not want to stretch anymore.

By that time, Brianna and Brittany were teens, and Brecca was nine. We enjoyed movie nights, had our Tex-Mex fix a couple of nights per week, and life was good. We still traveled a lot and poured into our girls, teaching them about their value and potential. We had always been quick to point to female role models and even hired female pilots for our jets. We wanted them to be positioned to take on the world with no limits. Stacye was always incredible at affirming them, and having increased time with my girls was something I was looking forward to. I had always prided myself on being able to see what was coming in business. However, something was coming to change our household that I had no vision for whatsoever.

- - -

It started during a trip to Vegas. Being a big gambler, our suite was comped at the Wynn, and we were set for a great evening. I got dressed up, shook on my gold Patek Phillipe watch, and headed to the bar for a drink while Stacye finished getting ready.

As I sat at the bar, a guy walked up next to me and ordered his. He was tan, Italian-looking, with a nice suit and a big watch. He was an OG, like me.

"Where are you from?"

"Dallas. You?"

"New York. Your watch is beautiful," he said.

"Thanks—yours too."

His wife approached, and they had to run.

"It was great to meet you. Enjoy your night."

The next morning, I was in the steam room and recognized him. He noticed me, too.

"Hey, how you doin'? I remember seeing you last night," he said. "Did you guys have a good time?"

"We did, as always."

I had been in there for 18 minutes, so I got out before I passed out. Plus, I wasn't in the mood for a long conversation.

I grabbed a juice and sat down. Ten minutes later, he

came out and sat down next to me. He started talking to me... and talking to me... and talking to me some more. He went on and on about a car business he used to own, his wife who left him, his cocaine addiction, his affairs, his five children who disowned him, his friendship with the San Diego mayor, and so on. Bear in mind, I was doing absolutely *nothing* to egg this guy on. He just would not shut up.

In my head, I thought, *He wants to borrow money, or he wants me to invest in his car business or something. There has to be an ask. Why else would he tell me all this?*

The conversation went on for at least 35 minutes. Under any normal circumstance, I would have just left. As you have gathered so far in the book, I had no problem being blunt with people. Yet I was glued. I just stayed there. Finally, after almost an hour of listening, I looked at my watch.

"Hey man, I've got to take off."

"Before you go, listen, Mike, I've got my wife back, my business back, my kids respect me, I've got money again, and I'm off drugs."

Well, that's a shift in the narrative.

He continued, "Here's the reason why: I gave my life to Jesus Christ. He is my Lord and Savior." He then went on for another 15 minutes, telling me about how great his life is now that he follows Jesus.

I thought he was a wack job.

"God bless you, bro, sounds great."

I left and could not help but think, *Why did I sit there and listen to this nut job evangelical for an hour?*

I got on the elevator, and I thought, *I'm not telling Stacye any of this.* I could just hear her saying, "Mike, this is a sign from God!" I rolled my eyes just thinking about it. I walked into the hotel room and the first thing that came out of my mouth was, "Stacye, you're not going to believe what just happened to me..." I recalled the entire thing to her. She, of course, started reading the tea leaves.

I felt like religion created a massive separation between the church and the world I was living in. They always seemed to have an agenda and always seemed to be fake. In fact, I remember having dinner with the pastors of the church we attended, and the pastor said she did not even believe that Jesus was Lord. I had to pick Stacye's jaw up off the floor after that comment. I was not shocked in the least. It was all a big farce anyway, or so I thought.

CHAPTER TWELVE

YOU'RE WELCOME

WE RETURNED TO Dallas after a nice time in Vegas. By then, my brother and I had long been reconciled. I called him up. "Hey, come over on a Tuesday and we'll go to the lake, cook some steaks, and drink beer." He came over and we started the two-hour drive to Possum Kingdom. He began to tell me about a hard time he was going through in his personal life. I'll spare the details, but I made a crude comment, which was not out of the ordinary for me. He said, "I don't think like that anymore." *Interesting,* I thought. He elaborated.

"Over the last few years, I've really been giving my life to Jesus. I've changed."

Man. This God stuff is not leaving me alone.

"I can see you're searching, Mike. There's a book called *The Same Kind of Different as Me* by Ron Hall. You should check it out."

"Ok, I'll read it."

I read it. It really impacted me. I remember reading the book on the airplane and weeping. I recall a scene in which a Christian woman was dying. A non-believing Jewish friend came to visit as she was passing, and he saw angels surrounding her bed. He converted to Christ as a result. This particular scene, for reasons beyond my understanding at the time, touched me deeply. Stacye also read it and loved it.

Somehow I was being primed for something more. I was being emotionally tenderized. I started to think more about the whole church thing and even developed a deeper interest. Someone said, "You should check out *Watermark Church*."

We patronized the place one Sunday and liked the vibe. It was different from the Methodist church we had attended and was certainly different from my Catholic upbringing. It seemed relevant and interesting. I was by no means a Christian, but I was also no longer a *cynic*. I was *curious*.

At around that time, a watershed moment happened. My oldest daughter got really sick. She was 18 at the time. We took her to the pediatrician, who quickly directed us to take her to the hospital. We sat there for 8 hours waiting while tests were being done and care was being administered. They finally released her on a clean bill of health to recover at home. We got home at around 6 p.m. My mom, who always had New-Age leanings, used to say, "Thank God in all circumstances." With that reminder surfacing, I decided to try it. I sat outside, looked up at the sky, and said, "Thank You, God, for saving Brittany." I probably said, "Thank You, God," for an hour straight.

It really did not occur to me that I was actually *praying*. I just felt genuine gratitude and expressed it. I didn't even think much about *who* I was talking to. Was it God? The Universe? Jesus? Thor?

I went to bed that night and had a dream. Sure, I had dreams occasionally, but nothing noteworthy and nothing I would read into. Yet, in this particular dream, I felt a strange sense of power. It was huge. It was like being in a room with a lion, but I was not able to see the lion. I was fearful, yet not scared. I was intimidated by how strong this power was, but not to the point of panic. Then, I heard a voice. It spoke something to me, but in a different language. I had no clue what it meant, but it made an impression on me.

The next morning, I described it to Stacye.

"You should talk to your brother about it," she recommended.

I dialed him.

"Can we meet for coffee?"

"Sure thing."

I walked him through the entire back story. I told him what had happened with Brittany and the events that happened afterward.

"You know how mom always told us to thank God in every circumstance?"

"Yeah."

"Well, I did. I must have thanked God a few hundred times."

I then walked him through the dream in detail. My brother and I had walked through business strategy many times in the boardroom. We had uncovered market opportunities and hashed out corporate issues more than once. Deciphering spiritual dreams was new territory for us.

"What did the voice say?" he asked.

In the best and most accurate way I could, I repeated the foreign words I had heard in my dream.

"Oh... oh wow." His eyes began to fill with tears. "Mike, that's Latin..."

For what? I thought.

"It's Latin, and it means *you're welcome.*"

Tears. Both of us had plenty by that point. My hundreds of *thank yous* had been answered... and in a way that I could not deny.

I had spent my life up until that point trying to be a master salesman, making pitches and drawing in clients, but the roles had switched without me knowing it. I was now the prospect. I had been courted. I had been pursued. I was in the mousetrap. Heaven made the pitch. God had extended the offer. I was on the receiving end of the most beautiful five-point close imaginable. I could not deny it. God had won me.

I prayed with Matt and gave my life to Jesus that day.

- - -

That night I called Matt and thanked him.

"No... thank you, Mike. You have no idea. There are 11,000 people celebrating right now."

"How so?"

"We have an email prayer chain with 11,000 people, and for the past four years, we've been praying for you to come to Jesus."

It was overwhelming. It was crazy. I realized later that God allowed him to have a front-row seat to my conversion. I was beginning to see that the Jesus of the Bible looked and sounded different than the caricature of Jesus that I had seen growing up in church. I opened up the

Bible and sobbed because I *understood* it. Prior to making Jesus my Lord, the Bible was all hieroglyphics. It did not make sense to me. Yet now, I was reading it, grasping it, and applying it.

I was excited to go back to church, not as a skeptic, cynic, or curious bystander—but as an actual Christian. "I accepted Jesus Christ as my Lord and Savior," I told one of the pastors. I could not believe what I was hearing coming out of my mouth. I had been a hardshell tycoon who hated evangelicals. What was happening to me? For several months, it felt like someone else was in my body speaking things that I *would never* have said before. It was *so* surreal and bizarre to hear my own voice saying those things, but I couldn't deny what was happening. God was changing me actively.

Prior to that, if I saw a born-again type, I would wreck my car trying to run them over. Yet when I came around true, authentic Christians, I thought, *Oh my gosh... I love these guys. They have real sins, real problems, and real issues.* It was not shots of King James Bible with a fire and brimstone chaser. It was a group that understood the love, grace, and heart of Jesus. I became fully aware that God was not trying to smite me. I also understood that Christians were not some odd bunch with no relatability. In fact, we met so many level-headed, affluent, and wonderful people in our church who also shared a common faith in Jesus. My eyes were being opened quickly and in a big way. I had experienced a *road to Damascus moment,* but instead of being knocked off a horse, I was knocked off a Bentley. Keep in mind, it did not happen in an instant. Everything from my Vegas encounter to the dream, to the conversations that followed all set me up for a change that took months.

Shortly after all of this unfolded, I had lunch with Todd Wagner, pastor at Watermark, and some of his leadership team. We were enjoying lunch at Houston's in Dallas. I shared my conversion story with all of these seasoned Christians. I told them everything from my upbringing to my dream. When I shared about the Vegas incident, they all said, "Oh, that man was a Jesus-hound!" They all had language for this stuff—I didn't. I just knew what happened.

There were about five of us at the table. When I got to the climax of my testimony, I looked around and all of the men were crying. It made me cry, too. I said to the men afterward, "Sorry, I'm so excited. I hope I wasn't too loud."

He replied, "McIntyre... we *live* for these moments."

For the first 90 days following my salvation, my life was like the movie *Limitless*. It felt like I could see around corners. It was beautiful. I felt compelled to tell everyone about what had happened to me—including my family. Stacye obviously got to witness the entire ordeal pan out and was eternally grateful for it. She had prayed for me for years, and those prayers had paid off. Within 30 days of my conversion, my whole family lined up like baby ducks following daddy, and my girls also gave their hearts to Jesus.

I was not walking around anymore. I was floating. Housekeepers would come in, and I would dance with them and make jokes. It freaked them out because that sort of levity had never been my norm. They blushed and my girls thought it was hilarious to see me out of character and childlike. The truth is, I was becoming more *me* than I had ever been. I was on fire, gobbling up sermons and learning this new tool called prayer. I began reaching out to other Christian men, and we started hosting *cigar, scotch, and Scripture* nights at our house. Sixty-plus guys would show up. We would get real and get right. It was wonderful.

This newfound community was so tight-knit. I sought out other believers and loved the fellowship. I remember being at a cocktail party with around 200 people in the house. Our friend's wife, Patty, was there, and I knew she was a believer. While she was in conversation with someone, I walked up behind them and began peeking over their shoulder, grinning at Patty, excited to talk to her about our now common faith. She smiled when she saw me, we talked and shared, and she later wrote me a beautiful card that brought tears to my eyes.

I was on cloud nine, but the thing about clouds is they don't always last long. When the 90-day boost wore off, my faith very much remained but would be tested. I was about to enter a trying season, not short on difficulty. My pastor advised me, "The enemy saw a big fish leaving the pond. You can expect a fight."

CHAPTER THIRTEEN

PLUGGING IN

WHEN IT RAINS, it pours. What they don't tell you is that sometimes it pours for months. In my case, it was nine months. Every area of my life seemed to come under attack: business, relationships, mental health, and then some. Disney on ice was over. We were now in the trenches doing battle. I remember thinking, *This is not good... but I'm going to stick with God's plan through this. Period.* The only thing I knew to do was to keep showing up. I got myself to church every Sunday and continued to weather the storm.

A good portion of my stress was wrapped up in selling my company. As I mentioned earlier, I was mentally out of the building when it came to my business. I was already checking out due to burnout, and coming to Jesus only amplified my disinterest. An offer was put on the table to acquire the company, and that was later taken away. It was back and forth with ups and downs. I sat in my car and wept at times.

I was biting my nails over how to handle the exit. I was nervous about selling at the wrong time. Imagine buying a stock, then that stock increases by $100,000, and before you sell, it then drops to $50,000. Did you lose $50,000? In a way—but really, you still gained $50,000. In my case, I was troubled about waiting too long to sell and coming up short of what I should have gotten out of the company I had spent years building.

Anxiety hit me throughout the day. It was all overwhelming. There were days that I could not bring myself to go into the office, and so Stacye would go in for me to take care of what needed to be buttoned up. She was so helpful in that season, and so was my brother Matt.

"Are you exercising?" Matt asked.

"I haven't in a little while," I admitted.

"Get back to exercising. It will help. Also, read Psalm 112 every day."

Psalm 112 became a pillar for me during that season:

"Surely the righteous will never be shaken; they will be remembered forever. They will have no fear of bad news; their hearts are steadfast, trusting in the Lord." (Psalm 112:6-7 NIV)

I learned to be vulnerable in those months. Up until that point, I had feared showing weakness of any kind. My hard-knock business background taught that showing weakness was certain death. My new worldview taught that showing weakness was the only means of gaining strength. When I expose my weakness to God, He reveals His strength to me. I joined a faith-based business group called C12 and opened up to them. They prayed over me and encouraged me.

The exit strategy was becoming more and more clear. I sold the company and all my stock for a lucrative sum.

Waking up after I was out of the business seemed surreal. I had always assumed I would sell insurance until they threw dirt on my face. It took time for me to realize that you don't have to be *doing something* all the time. It took a total of six months to adjust to the new lifestyle. We went to Europe for 30 days and toured Scotland, Ireland, France, and Italy. Upon returning, I noticed that once you're out of the business, you're out. You have this idea that everyone else is going to stop their lives, too, but they don't. They keep on going. I felt like I was sitting on the sidelines, but it was where I needed to be. *What's next?* became my burning question.

I got the bug to pioneer again about a year after exiting the industry. We started a telemedicine program, worked on some benefits companies, and even built a business that enabled people to work from home. These odds and ends startups were great outlets for my entrepreneurial drive. We made money and are still earning revenue on some of those companies, and on others, we lost. That's the nature of venture capital.

- - -

My spiritual life was maturing at Watermark. It was a solid place for me to onramp. Todd Wagner was a hard-nosed pastor and an amazing Bible teacher. I recall him getting ticked on stage a time or two when the ProPresenter software would fail during a sermon. While some thought he could be nicer, I appreciated the straightforward approach, and I could relate to his demeanor.

We had lunch a time or two, and I was eventually invited to a private Bible study that he led. I asked Todd if I could bring my brother along. "Yeah, bring him in!" Todd encouraged. Matt showed up with me and didn't realize it was a private Bible study with the Senior Pastor. Todd would give everyone assignments and gladly held our feet to the fire if needed. He had no problem getting in your face and calling you out if you were sloppy. The very first week that Matt and I showed up, Todd looked at one of the guys in the group and said, "Jim, do you have the verse for us?"

The guy stuttered and stammered. He hadn't memorized his Scripture. He then took to defending himself.

"I just... I get nervous when you call me out like that, Pastor."

Todd was merciless. "Nervous, huh? That's because you are NOT PREPARED!"

The guy was getting thoroughly chewed out at 7 a.m. *Was I back in the military?* Afterward, as Matt and I hopped on the elevator to leave, he said, "I'm calling my secretary and canceling *all* of my appointments today. I'm memorizing every one of these frickin' Scriptures before next week."

From then on, we referred to Todd as the "Jack Bauer of Bible Study" for obvious reasons.

The church environment was healthy. It was a large gathering of stable believers who had good socioeconomic standing. I was continuing to learn and develop as a new Christian. My heart was 100% in, but at times it felt like my logical, business mind was skeptical. I had questions that lingered and surfaced occasionally. *Why Jesus? Is He the only way? What about other faiths?* These questions were settled and then some about a year into my journey when a gentleman named Lee Strobel showed up to speak at Watermark.

I had no clue who he was at the time, but discovered quickly that he had lots of acclaim among Christians. He was a former atheist and investigative journalist who had set out to debunk the biblical claims about Christ. As he dug into his investigation, he saw more and more evidence that Christ was exactly who He said He was. He converted to the faith and wrote the classic book, *The Case for Christ*. His sermon, layer by layer, answered my looming questions. Most sermons appealed to my heart; his appealed to both my heart *and* my logical mind.

My faith had a new type of strength and confidence because of Lee's visit. I was fully persuaded that what I now believed about God and life was not the result of pure emotion but the result of a very real, practical, and tangible God. Other speakers like Dinesh D'Souza also came and further cemented my new worldview.

We found ourselves volunteering at the church and we plugged in as active members. We served community projects and donated our time, talent, and treasure. Our entire family was enjoying the collateral benefits of being believers and being a part of something bigger than ourselves.

We liked to sit in the first two or three rows in church. It made everything up close and personal. We met a young guy named Blake, who was on the worship team and was hired every year to do the church's Christmas special. He was crazy talented, played a million instruments, and toured with *For King & Country*. Apparently, my oldest daughter caught his eye. They met and about a year later began dating.

We came to know him and love him. It was obvious

that he was good for Brittany, and she was good for him. Eventually, he had a *sit down* with me in my study and wanted to talk about the future. Of course, I knew what was coming. He walked me through where he was with his career and all that. I wasn't overly interested in what he was earning. A good FICO score wouldn't be enough for Brittany, but a good heart would—and he had one. When the question came, I gave him the green light to marry my firstborn daughter.

They had a beautiful wedding on Mackinac Island in Michigan, one of the girls' favorite spots growing up. It was not long after their marriage that Stacye and I found out we were grandparents-to-be. We were elated. When our grandson was born, it was a full house in the delivery room. Blake, Stacye, Brianna, Brecca, Blake's mom, and I were all in there. I stood back at a safe distance.

When the birth happened, a photo was snapped. We were all praying and worshipping Jesus, celebrating this new life. It was surreal and magical watching my own child step into motherhood. Within a year, Brittany was pregnant with a little girl. As the two grandbabies began talking, our names changed. I became Mac, and Stacye became Lala.

We have reaped ridiculous benefits from this thing called the Christian life. It has enriched and enhanced everything about *everything*. All of our daughters are here in Dallas. They all have degrees and are doing well. Brittany and Blake own a record label. Brianna is our organization's COO (a.k.a. the boss lady). And Brecca was bitten with the entrepreneurial bug, like me, and created a successful firm, Luxe Supply, here in Dallas.

Everywhere I look within our family, I see blessings upon blessings. Whether I leave 5 dollars or 5 billion, the character legacy we leave behind is the most important inheritance we can give. God has so aggressively gifted us with joys beyond words. It turns out, this whole faith thing was more than Father Rob's boring homilies. It was more than my stepmom's dogmatic religion. It was more than mean nuns and fanatical Baptists. It was about one person: Jesus.

CHAPTER FOURTEEN

CEO, AGAIN

"HEY MIKE, I hear you're going to Watermark... you know they don't believe in the gifts, right?"

"I don't know what you're talking about, man. They cash my gift every week."

It turns out, my brother's friend was referring to the gifts of the Holy Spirit, a Bible doctrine I hadn't brushed up on. We attended Watermark for six years, and during that time, I focused on the core values of what I believed, which was that Jesus was God, He died, was raised from the dead, and that salvation was given to anyone who bought in. I knew from business that if the fundamentals were not in order, nothing else would be. Eventually, though, Stacye and I became curious about jumping into the deep end.

A neighbor had mentioned that she was visiting a fledgling church called Upperroom. "The pastor is really amazing and authentic. He's young but sincere... he's the real deal." We were intrigued. We knew it was a charismatic-style church but didn't know much else. I had seen clips of Benny Hinn-style meetings and thought it was wacky. I didn't know whether bodies would be lying everywhere in the sanctuary or if rattlesnakes were going to be whipped out during worship. Nevertheless, we went.

The differences between Upperroom (UR) and Watermark smacked us in the face from the time we pulled into the parking lot. UR was located in a rented space above a Veterinary clinic. Watermark had a first-class campus worth tens of millions. I wasn't a fan of the aesthetic downgrade, but God knew I needed to get over myself. If Watermark was a 5-star hotel, UR was a manger. Watermark had a pretty homogenous congregation, whereas UR was maxed out with diversity, which we loved. Watermark was a mega-church. UR had about 150 people.

During our first service in attendance, I immediately noticed how free-flowing the culture was. I had gotten accustomed to Watermark's formulaic approach: 18-minutes of worship, 5-minutes of announcements, and a 40-minute sermon capped with a closing prayer. At Upperroom, worship alone went on for over an hour. I struggled with that at first. I glanced up at the stage and saw a few really young guys leading worship. None of them looked like they had ever filed a tax return. They were kids.

I looked around the room and saw people raising their hands, singing loud, and a handful of them shook with charismania. It was different... but I wasn't turned off by it. It was free in there. The very first night, there was a fire tunnel[1] and my daughter was part of it, laying

---

[1] A fire tunnel is a prayer line where one can walk through and receive prayer from others. Think of it like the church version of a basketball team running through a tunnel of cheerleader pom poms as they take to the court.

hands on others in prayer. My family was diving in head first. I was still skeptical over the long worship set until the pastor, Michael Freeland Miller, stood up and made a statement.

"Worship is a muscle. It has to be built over time. I know some of you aren't used to worship going on for this long... but you need to know that the sermon is for you, but worship is for Him."

Until that moment, I had never put two and two together, that the songs we sing were not for our entertainment. They were not just spiritual calisthenics to loosen us up for the message. No, worship is *for God, and God alone.* His comment really helped me to shift my take on the subject and I grew to appreciate those extended times of worship.

When we returned to the car after a 3-hour long service, I thought for sure Brecca, who at the time was 14, would have said, "Meh." Instead, when I turned around and asked, "What did you think?" she looked at me with all seriousness and said, "Daddy, I had an awakening." Well, that was it. We were now going to Upperroom.

We felt it was time to plant our flags and call UR our home church. I did visit Watermark several Sundays later after the Upperroom, just to see if I made the correct decision. I immediately saw that I did. Stacye loved it, our girls loved it, and I did, too. The charismatic circle helped me to see things I hadn't seen prior. I became aware that Jesus is not short on grace and love. His tank is overflowing with both.

In past church experiences, I had seen plenty of legalism and performance-based Christianity. This new church life was introducing me to a side of God that has always existed, but I had not seen. The tenth verse of the tenth chapter of John's gospel became my life verse:

> "The thief comes only to steal and kill and destroy; I have come that they may have life, and have it to the full." (John 10:10 NIV)

What did Jesus mean when He said He gives us life *to the full?* What does this abundance look like? I had experienced some aspects of abundance in my life and career—the financial gain, the means to help others, the wonderful family. God had always been working. Yet I lacked an *internal abundance* that only God was fit to supply.

When I gave myself to Jesus, He took a holistic approach to my life, leaving nothing unchanged. He was growing the good and pruning the bad, a process that is still very much continuing.

As we plugged in at UR, I began enjoying worship in new ways. I felt free to dance down front, cry at the goodness of God, and be *fully me.* I wasn't flopping around like a carp on the ground. I refuse to manufacture manifestations—but I was embracing the church culture and loving it. I recall folks coming up to me and praying in tongues over me in church. I had no issue with it because I saw it in the Bible.

However, speaking in a spiritual language just didn't happen for me in church. Instead, it happened for me on a run. It was a hot summer day in Dallas. I found myself with hands raised, worshipping the Lord, when out of my mouth came another language. It flowed and has ever since. Yep. The harsh, cynical millionaire tycoon had become a bonafide tongue-talking lover of Jesus. If God is not real, the only way that transformation could have happened was if someone had a gun to my head, but nobody did, and God is very much the real deal.

When reading the first and second parts of this book, it might seem like I am talking about two completely different people. That's because I am. We sometimes say there was a "night and day difference," but that phrase doesn't adequately express the contrast between my old and new life. If someone had told me in 1995 that I would one day be worshipping Jesus and praying publicly, I would have laughed them out of the boardroom.

Some have the misconception that when you come to Jesus, you become a solemn, boring, dry, lifeless person. The complete opposite of that is the truth. When you come to Jesus, the excitement truly begins. Food tastes better, jokes are funnier, a round of golf is more enjoyable, and life as a whole is amplified. Are there seasons of difficulty? Of course. But this life is more *glory* than it is *grind*.

The overall theme of the gospel is that enjoying Jesus positions us to enjoy everything else to the full. God has a way of optimizing every part of you and your world. He doesn't throw out your unique experiences and gifts. He utilizes them.

My time in the corporate world was not lost time. In fact, in many ways, I see it as preparation for my ultimate calling. After being settled and established at UR for some time, it became known that I had business success and ample experience in pioneering organizations. Michael, who leads Upperroom, was 15 years younger than me and started pulling on my experience. Understandably, he had questions about leadership, organizational structure, and managing people. We had a great connection which facilitated great conversation. We golfed and traveled, and our wives loved each other.

I was being asked to consult and coach more and more. In the same way that Jack and Hal had poured into me as mentors, I began to pour out to my mentees. Being a builder and a motivator, I sometimes addressed the staff at Upperroom the same way I would address my sales teams.

"I don't know why this church out west is so popular. They are in a tiny town. There's no major airport. The main preacher is more boring than C-Span... but people flock to this place. We are in Dallas. We have the best preachers, the best worship leaders, and the best accessibility! We should be booming!"

I was later told some of the staff recoiled at my motivational speech. Sure, I was importing some corporate-style motivation, but who did they think they were getting? Nevertheless, Upperroom was good soil to sow into. I continued to share what I had, and they continued to soak it up.

- - -

"I want you to be my executive pastor on staff, and I want to pay you." Michael offered me the job at UR, and I had to think about my answer for a grand total of .00003 seconds.

"Listen, I'm glad to coach you from afar but that type of role is not me."

Some time later, he approached me again.

"You're amazing, Mike. I love what you have to offer. Would you come on board and oversee our staff?"

He was loving, caring, generous, gracious, and really touched my heart, but I had to turn him down again.

The third time around, I took his offer. I did it for one reason: I felt like God wanted me to.

"Let's do a 90-day deal. You can pay me a little money, and I'll come on board and help develop this thing."

When I go into something, I go in hook, line, and sinker. I don't do halfway. Working at Upperroom was no different. The first thing I did was set structure for employees. At the time, staff was coming in at ten and leaving at one. That changed quickly. I instituted grown-up workdays.

I then asked for job descriptions from every employee, and they about had cardiac arrest. Overall, they knew how to soak, but not how to sweep. They knew *adoration,* but not *administration.* My role was pouring basic concrete foundations for the organization. The staff tended to adapt quickly. My time building systems and efficiencies in the insurance world was now being used for God's kingdom.

When the 90-day contract was up, Michael said, "Let's do another 90."

"No, I'm not up for another 90. If we do this, I want the position of CEO. Here's the money I'll need, and we can move forward full time."

An agreement was made, and I was a CEO again. My plate was full from the start. The church had been shut down by the fire marshall because the space above the vet clinic couldn't support our growth. We needed a million dollars for a building upgrade, and the staff was unsure of how to go about hiring a contractor. I had built buildings in the past, so I spearheaded some of those areas.

I also immediately started implementing policies and procedures. The church was *free*, but lacked *form* on the staff end. We had desire, but very little capacity. When desire outweighs capacity, something is going to break. We created a skeleton and a structure. We increased salaries, balanced budgets, and started pioneering new aspects of the ministry. The church exploded with growth and expanded by 400%. We started a record label, began pushing high-quality video content, and put on incredible conferences. It was anything but a solo effort from me or any one person. The staff really engaged with what God was doing, and being a part of that was incredible.

Stacye and I eventually traveled to Denver to help plow the ground for a new UR campus. I don't recommend anyone start a church in Denver unless you have unlimited funds or people who are willing to fight 13 rounds every day for a decade. It's tough ground to plow for a church plant. No less, we involved ourselves in getting that church up and running, and it was an invaluable experience.

While we were there, we got word that things were heading south for my father's health. He was still back in Michigan. He and Betty had never left. His dementia was getting worse. He was in a nursing home after falling in a restaurant bathroom and knocking out teeth, as well as breaking his nose on the sink. My dad had always been a tough, strong man, so seeing him like that was hard to take.

Matt had traveled to Michigan to care for him. He really stepped up in that season, and we were grateful for it. With Dad's dementia chipping away at every part of his mind, we knew he would not last much longer. Matt called me while I was in Denver, "Dad is not doing good.

He isn't going to make it much longer, Mike. I'm here with him. I'll put the phone up to his ear if there is anything you'd like to tell him."

I took a deep breath.

"Dad, I love you. I miss you... and I forgive you for everything that's happened. I'm grateful that you will see Jesus soon."

He was not able to respond because of the state he was in, but my brother did say he raised his eyebrows when I said those things. I can only trust Jesus that my words found their way to some small part of him that was still in it. Within 24 hours, he left this world. I went to the airport with the pastor I had been working with to fly back to Michigan for the funeral.

"Jesus is going to welcome your father with open arms," the pastor said to me.

I wept. It was a tender moment.

Matt was gracious in doing the heavy lifting. My sister also flew up, and we did the funeral. My dad was by no means a great dad. He just wasn't. But he did what he could with what he was given. I loved him and definitely held some fond memories. The funeral was a great time to reconnect with siblings, laugh, and cry. We met some of his marine buddies and honored my father's life. His wife, Betty, went on to live for a few more years. When the memorial had wrapped up, and all had said their good-byes, it was back to the ministry.

- - -

Overall my style at UR was laissez faire. I wanted people to be free to flourish in their talents and abilities. We hired good people, set the parameters, and let them run.

If they didn't cut it, we would make adjustments. I really loved working with some of the pastors on staff, like Michael Mauldin and Peter Louis who were genuine go-getters. There are many others in the church I fully enjoyed and respected, but the list would be too long to rattle off here.

As my CEO tenure wore on, Michael would ask me, "Are you happy in this role?" To be perfectly honest, *I wasn't.* Sure, I had incredible times. The conferences we put on were first class, the staff retreats were unforgettable, and I loved the people. But at the end of the day, the role was very much *sacrificial.* It was hard. It was new. I had paused everything else in my business life to take the position. I was bearing my cross. That's not a bad thing—it was just reality. It's not a complaint, it's a confession. I was able to apply my business know-how to the nonprofit world, which was great, but it was an adjustment as I learned to quantify outcomes in a completely new way.

Being number two to Michael, the founder, was a humbling experience also. I had run the show in my enterprise for decades, so submitting my ideas and decisions to another person was trying. Michael was generous and fantastic. We butted heads at times, as leaders do, but our mutual respect and admiration won the day.

After 18 months on staff, I felt my run was ending. I had contributed what God wanted me to contribute, and it was time for the season to close. It was summertime, and Stacye and I hadn't taken a vacation in some time. We had worked a lot leading up to it and took a couple of weeks off. After we came back, I met with Michael, and he recommended that we begin the process of transitioning out, and I fully agreed. We both knew that my time on staff was not forever, so the transition was organic and came as no surprise to either of us.

Looking back, it was perfect timing. We had an off-site staff retreat in west Texas at a nice lake where I was able to say goodbye to the staff and part on excellent terms. I was ready to move on to what was next. It was probably harder on my family than it was for me. Brianna was working at UR at the time and continued on staff for a few months after my departure.

There are certain things that you take with you when a season wraps up. After a meeting with Goliath, David carried the head of a giant with him. After the exodus, Israel carried the wealth of Egypt with them. For me, I carried with me a desire to build a coaching and training organization.

Leading the staff retreats planted something within me that I couldn't shake. I told Stacye, "I think we should do some experiential learning with the staff." So we did. I walked them through exercises and programs that developed them personally and developed them as leaders. If Jesus took a holistic approach to my life when I got saved, I wanted to take a holistic approach with my clients.

At one of these retreats, Michael said to me, "This is revolutionary. You need to bring this out at scale." I couldn't help but feel the same way. As a result, we birthed the *Next Level Experience*.

CHAPTER FIFTEEN

NEXT LEVEL

YOUR HEART WILL go where your money is. If you are paying to have a meeting at 9 a.m. on Friday, you will be there at 9 a.m. on Friday. If you are not paying, the meeting is optional and could be easily bumped if something more interesting pops up. When we launched *McIntyre*, our coaching and training company, we kept this in mind. I knew that if we had clients who had to invest their dollars, their hearts would travel with the money and real change could happen.

It was shortly after my tenure at Upperroom that we began to structure my coaching business and formalize events like *Next Level Experience (NLE)* and *Leadership 300*, all under the *McIntyre* banner. I had one goal: to take people whose lives were already working and enable them to enter the next level—experiencing the abundant life from John 10:10 every single day. We had made up our minds from the start that we wouldn't be a counseling center for the broken. While those firms have great value, it just wasn't our gift. We aimed to offer a redemptive lift to those who wanted to go from *good to great*.

Over the past few years, we have poured countless hours and substantial personal capital into building these new platforms. I want to go big with it. I'm fond of the phrase, "Reach for the stars... because if all you do is catch the moon, you've done alright."

These days, the bulk of my time is spent with personal coaching clients and preparing for upcoming *McIntyre* events. When I start with a new potential client, we hop on a 30-minute call. In it, I'm asking questions, hearing where they are, and evaluating their goals and desires. It's like the work of a physician, without the stethoscope. We are listening to symptoms, uncovering root issues, and making habit prescriptions that are custom to each client.

From there, I send a proposal based on what I feel needs to happen. We keep things realistic and actionable. *McIntyre* is not a magic bullet. If someone wants to go from obscurity to world-famous in 30 days, I'm not their guy. However, if someone wants to intentionally alter their habits and set themselves up to attract John 10:10 realities into their life, we can help.

We take a deep dive into our client's lives. We come in at a 45-degree angle. We waste no time getting into the spiritual, relational, financial, and physical arenas. All four quadrants are connected. If your marriage is not right, it'll be hell trying to sustain a business. If you are spiritually starved, keeping your finances together can be a strain. It is holistic surgery.

The idea is that we want to move the needle *now*. I know some coaches will encourage a two-year program. That's fine, but it's not me. I'm a results man, and I want to see the shift happen ASAP. Do you need a raise at work? We will walk you through how to have that conversation, and that conversation will happen next week, not eight months from now when you've gone through my 32-week prep course. It's not necessarily instant gratification, but it is instant *action*.

Because of this fast and furious approach, I generally only coach people for 60 days with an absolute max stint of 90 days. After that, I mandate a 40-day break minimum. I do not want people to cling to me or become addicted to a program. I am not building a *crutch*, but rather a *bridge* that ultimately leads to Jesus.

Having a coach is like having someone to point out the cabbage stuck in your teeth after lunch. They find the obvious stuff that you would never have noticed otherwise. As a young CEO, one of the best decisions I made was to bring in consultants who did a *360 assessment* to evaluate how I showed up to my staff. They had all of my C-level staff and management do an anonymous survey of me. It was really good and it stung, too, as it should. It turns out, I was bold and authentic, but also too brash and blunt. Big surprise. This consultation enabled me to see my blind spots and add some sugar to my vinegar style of management.

With my clients, I am their biggest cheerleader, as well as teaching them to be their own cheerleader. When no one else is around to encourage you, encourage yourself. Growing up, my mother adhered to a cocktail mixture of biblical truth, a little Buddhism, and a little New Age. She taught me to practice positive affirmations. Throughout my life, from the time I was a teenager until today, I have clung to this practice. In the mirror, I have said things like, *I deserve to be prosperous. I have great worth. The only differ-*

ence between me and a multi-billionaire is while he is working on his second billion, I am working on my first. My mind is in touch with God's source of money-making power. I am a great husband. I am a great dad. I am learning to love well.

I now realize that these affirmations are entirely biblical. "You will also *declare* a thing, and it will be established for you" (Job 22:28 NKJV, emphasis added). I have taught my clients to adopt a culture of self-affirmation. You won't always have someone at your side to affirm you, so you have to step up and do it yourself.

At the same time, the program is not all coddling and comforting. We get real. I was recently on a call with a client, and it went something like this:

"How are your assignments going?"

There was a slight hesitation on the other end of the line.

"...I didn't do them. I'm traveling right now," they responded.

"Hmmm, let me say it delicately: I. Don't. Care. It's 2021. You can connect anywhere, anytime. Do you want to keep going with the program?"

"This is exactly why I'm paying you. I needed a kick in the pants. Thank you! I'll get on it. No excuses."

I do *not* coddle—I coach.

Beyond that, we are raising up other coaches. I am reproducing myself by certifying coaches who can reach exponential clients under our banner. In the insurance world, I protected my client's wealth and increased my salespeople's wealth. We created a number of millionaires. Now, our aim is to bring our coaches to the next level, and their clients will naturally join with them.

Our coaches are funneled through our programs like *NLE* and *Leadership 300*. From there, we vet them for commitment and willingness. What is their marriage like? What about their children? Are they spiritually sound? Do they have their finances in order? Once these things are answered in a way that satisfies, they go through a rigorous 3-month marine corps-style coaching bit. Some don't make it. It's not easy, but it is not intended to be easy. We aim to create coaches who know how to lead retreats, generate resources, and coach their clients with absolute excellence. From there, the money will come. Money is just the byproduct of excellence.

Since starting *McIntyre*, we have seen successful ministries birthed, marriages healed, books written, and fruit on display. The most common feedback we get from attendees is, "This is life-changing. I wish I would have done this earlier."

In the coming years, we want to see hundreds of coaches trained and certified, as well as increase our staff substantially. We want to tackle the practical and tackle the spiritual in a holistic, dual-focused program. We also have a vision to expand our offerings to the nations. I try not to be too specific with my goals. Goals can be overrated. First, if you don't reach them, you might be disheartened and quit altogether. Second, goals can limit possibilities. They sometimes act as a cap. If you say, "I want to hit my goal of $5,000 in sales this week," and you hit that number, you might put your feet up and pat yourself on the back. Yet in reality, you could have hit $20,000 had you not pumped the brakes at $5,000.

Nevertheless, I do have *vision*. I see where we are going. Like a movie, I have watched the direction the organization is headed—and it is *up*. We are going to continue to uncover strengths and bolster weaknesses with our clients. When we get people to do the things they don't want to do, see things they don't want to see, and hear what they don't want to hear, they will become who God meant them to be.

Like with any venture I have pursued, our coaching and training organization has not been without trial. At the start of 2020, we had been hosting *Next Level Experiences* for about six years. We were growing, ramping up the events, and set to host them in hotels. When the pandemic hit, we came face to face with a hard choice. *How do we proceed?*

The hotel we had booked for our April event was off limits, but our home was available. Driven by a mandate to equip and train leaders, we made the choice to open our home and continue to host events. If folks weren't comfortable with the risk, it was no problem at all to cancel. Yet for those who wanted to come, our doors were open. We had eight NLE's in 2020 with between 25 and 40 people per event. We did not have a single case of Covid contracted with any attendees, by the grace of God. Our organization continued to put out content and expand.

During that season, most churches resorted to online services. We found an Episcopalian church that was gathering in person and attended. It was a joy to experience a church service that resembled the Catholic upbringing I had. I saw Christ at the heart of it in ways that I never noticed prior to coming to Jesus. Plus, we got a kick out of the incense that was burned in the service. "I feel like I'm either in a forest fire or in a Cheech & Chong movie," I joked to Stacye.

We also enjoyed connecting online with churches. I overheard Stacye listening to a preacher online and I inquired.

"Who's that?"

"Tracy Eckert."

I had known of her through working at Upperroom. We had mutual connections. She was pastoring at Storehouse Church in Dallas and I decided to attend. I visited in October of 2020 and loved what I felt. I could see the leadership was like-minded, I connected with their backgrounds, and the Word and worship were superb.

A few days after visiting, I got a message from Tracy asking if I would coach her and her team. My engagement with Upperroom still felt fresh, so I had very little interest in consulting with a church again. Nevertheless, we met, found ourselves on the same page, and I sent a proposal. A month later, they accepted and I began advising in the church leadership space yet again. This time, though, it was completely different than my tenure at UR. The demographics, the nature of the work, and the type of engagement were drastically different. It was refreshing. It was reinvigorating. It was like falling in love with the church again.

- - -

Risk and *faith* are synonymous. I had gotten accustomed to risk in the business world for years, but didn't realize that faith was the exact same thing. I fell in love with the high of cashing in on risk. I have felt that high more times than I felt failure in my career. I don't want to live with regrets. I don't want to sit around asking, *Why didn't I take the shot? Why didn't I go for it?* Since my conversion, I have felt the high of reaping benefits from *faith* also. Stacye and I have been so blessed to step out and pioneer something with a third man at the table, Jesus.

I am a Vegas guy. I enjoy the tables—sue me (it

wouldn't be the first time). I've found if you go in with *scared money that you cannot lose*, you will lose it all. If you go in with *entertainment money to have fun with*, losing is a secondary concern. More often than not, if you go in with that mentality, you do better than you would otherwise. I have tried over the years to give myself the freedom to fail, which is actually the freedom to learn. If I bet the farm, I always made sure I could rebuild the farm if I needed to.

It has never been easier to step out in faith and make your move. When you step out in faith according to God's plan, you can only lose what God did not want you to have anyway. With $500, you can build a business with just you and your dog in the garage, but your website looks like you have been in business since the Reagan administration. It does not take much to get started. Start with little. Hunger *creates* creativity. If you have a cash cushion, don't rest on your laurels. Force yourself to earn.

Entrepreneurs create something from nothing. They work like no one else for the next five years to live like no one else forever. They don't fear a white blank page. They show up and build it better, faster, and cheaper. They make people's lives better, healthier, prettier, and wealthier—and the money they make is just a byproduct of that pursuit.

Ronald Reagan was a personal hero of mine, and I learned from him greatly. When he ran for governor and eventually for president, he always ran as though he was 20 points behind his opponent. I adopted that mentality. My father-in-law and I were at lunch after a huge week. I had sold like crazy and expected to get an *atta boy* from him. Instead, he said, "Son, now you need to pour the coals on the fire." I thought, *Ok... now we are playing in the big leagues. We don't settle.*

From then on, if I made $20,000 in a week, I acted as though I lost $20,000. If an accountant said, "We are in the black this quarter, Mike," my brain translated it to, "We are severely in the red this quarter, Mike." This irked my staff, but they understood why I was successful. They just didn't always like how I went about it.

I operated as though I was running 20% behind. In reality, though, in a spiritual sense, I was 100% behind and had no way to climb my way back. I needed a Savior. I needed Christ, the bonafide CEO of heaven and earth, to coach me, grow me, change me, and save me. God had looked out for me from my early days on the snowy Michigan streets to my corporate days in a corner office. However, it was not until I looked back at Him that my world did a 180, and I was introduced to a brand of prosperity that I did not know was possible.

- - -

I am often asked, "Why have you shifted your efforts to running a coaching firm?"

"*God,*" would be the short three-letter answer.

The longer answer is that we are in love with the possibility of seeing hearts and lives changed. Very few things excite me as much as standing in front of a roomful of clients, pouring my heart out in candid, vulnerable communication. Communication is the most powerful force we have. It is how God changes man and how man changes his world.

My brother said many years ago, "Michael says the things we all wish we could say, but don't say them." Let me button up this book by saying what needs to be said. People write memoirs for a number of reasons. It could be legacy, money, or even boredom. Personally, the work on this book was not commenced because I needed something else to do. It was not filler for the schedule. I've laid out my life journey in the hope that it acts as an elevator for you, taking you from the level you are on to the level you belong. What happens next is in your hands.

Are you ready to go to *the next level*?

MICHAEL McINTYRE built a $3 billion dollar agency from scratch, having recruited over 20,000 sales agents and developed a unique set of training techniques that revolutionized the industry. Michael is a corporate and individual coach. He has helped many C-Suite executives, entrepreneurs and business professionals positively transform their lives. Michael has worked with the *Dallas Cowboys, American Equity Life Insurance Co., Puritan Financial* and many other kinds of organizations.

As a coach, Michael takes a holistic approach to bring out the best in your life spiritually, relationally, and financially. Michael creates individualized programs for those of you who want to experience growth and see greater results. As a coach, Michael specializes in deep diving into the area(s) where you want to experience transformation.

For more information or to get involved with
coaching and events visit:

THEMICHAELMCINTYRE.COM

ENDNOTE

1 Sullivan, Brian. "Job Losses since 9/11 Attacks Top 2.5 Million." Computerworld, Computerworld, 25 Mar. 2003, www.computerworld.com/article/2581548/job-losses-since-9-11-attacks-top-2-5-million.html.

For information on bulk ordering this title,
contact the publisher at:

TALLPINEBOOKS.COM